New Every Morning

**An Extraordinary Women Study into the
Goodness and Mercy of God**

Julie Clinton & Megan Allison
with Dina Jones

Unless otherwise noted, biblical passages are from The Holy Bible, English Standard Version. ESV® Text Edition: 2016. Copyright © 2001 by Crossway Bibles, a publishing ministry of Good News Publishers.

Passages marked NIV are from The Holy Bible, New International Version®, NIV® Copyright © 1973, 1978, 1984, 2011 by Biblica, Inc.® Used by permission. All rights reserved worldwide.

ISBN: 978-1-960624-16-1

Cover design by Kimberly Witte Bailey
Interior layout by Anne McLaughlin, Blue Lake Design

Published by American Association of Christian Counselors Publishing
Printing in the United States

One of the very first verses I (Julie) learned as a child was Psalm 119:11, "Thy word have I hid in my heart that I might not sin against you." Those early days in Sunday School began a journey into my love for God's Word. I try to start each day spending time with the Lord anchored in the scriptures as a "lamp unto my feet, and a light unto my path."

Our prayer is that God will fill your heart as we study His Word together in *New Every Morning*. Our hope is that you will be encouraged, strengthened and challenged to live free in Christ.

Contents

As We Begin . . .

**Surely goodness and mercy shall follow me
all the days of my life . . .**

IN DAVID'S MOST BEAUTIFUL PSALM, he describes times of peace and plenty as well as seasons of opposition and hardship. In each case, he reminds us how a loving, attentive shepherd cares for the flock. God leads us to still waters where it's easy to quench our thirst; He restores our souls when we feel anxious; He leads us, protects us, comforts us, and spreads a lavish table before us when we need nourishment. In David's time, hosts anointed their guests with oil as a sign of love and honor, and God anoints us as He welcomes us into His presence each day. The love, kindness, protection, and provision make David's heart burst, and we can almost hear him shout, "My cup overflows!" After reviewing God's affectionate and constant care, even in the midst of difficulties, David concludes, "Surely goodness and mercy shall follow me all the days of my life, and I shall dwell in the house of the Lord forever" (Psalm 23).

As we've met thousands of women at Extraordinary Women events, we've witnessed people with David's perspective on life—in joyful times, confusing times, and times of heartache. They've faced their fears, dug deep to tap into the vast reservoirs of God's power and love, and found the courage to trust Him with the next step . . . and the next. A life of faith is challenging, but a life without faith is a disaster.

In this study, we want to share what we've learned about finding the treasure of God's goodness and mercy in the challenges we all face. Time after time, God invites us to lean on His wisdom, care, and power when we feel we're running on empty. We all face difficulties in our health, finances, most important relationships, and the challenge of finding God in dark times. Our prayer is that God will lead us as we walk the path David walked, hear God when He calls to us when we wander, and realize He is supremely trustworthy. With each step, we'll say, "Surely goodness and mercy shall follow me all the days of my life."

This Bible study was written by both of us, Julie and Megan, mother and daughter. We've poured our hearts into this entire study. Because we use personal anecdotes, sometimes it's necessary to clarify which author is speaking, so in each week's study, we will identify the primary writer. But let's be clear about where credit is due: to paraphrase Psalm 127:1, "Unless the Lord writes the book, its authors labor in vain."

This Bible study is eight weeks long, with five days of reading, reflection, and prayer each week. The goal isn't to complete each reading and fill in the answers as quickly as possible. You don't get extra points for speed! Instead, ask God to open your heart to Him and His Word before you start each day's reading. When you feel the prompting of the Spirit to think, praise, give thanks, confess, or pray, respond with a willing heart. Some of us will want to write a lot more than the space provided, so use a journal to record your reflections.

Both of us pray that you'll experience more of God's goodness and mercy than ever before. That's what God wants for you; we're sure of that.

Julie and Megan

WEEK 1

The Source
of Goodness

Julie Clinton

For many of us, our first reflection on the goodness of God came from a recited prayer before meals: "God is great; God is good. Let us thank Him for our food." Our families bowed our heads at the table to thank God for what He had provided. Each recitation was a reminder of the goodness of our heavenly Father. It's something we are taught to acknowledge at an early age, yet how often do most people think about what it means that God is *good*? What does it mean that His goodness and mercy will surely follow us all the days of our lives (Psalm 23:6)?

In current terminology, "good" might have different meanings. To be told you did a good job means the assignment was well done, yet it doesn't necessarily indicate that you're upholding any moral standard. Then again, if you classify someone as a "good" person, you're suggesting that she is honest, fair, trustworthy, and morally upright.

So which meaning do we have in mind when we affirm that *God* is good? Certainly, we can be certain that everything He does is done to perfection. In the beginning, when "the earth was without form and void, and darkness was over the face of the deep" (Genesis 1:2), every phase of God's creation was acknowledged as "good" by God himself—the highest possible standard. Each day of creation was followed by God's assessment that His creation was good: the light on day 1, the separation of earth and sky on day 2, the vegetation on day 3, the sun, moon, and stars on day 4, birds and fish on day 5, and livestock and wild animals on day 6 (Genesis 1:4, 10, 12, 18, 21, 25). But also on day 6, after God had created Adam in His own image and breathed into him the breath of life, He noted that all He had made was *very* good (Genesis 1:31).

Yet Scripture also reveals that it isn't just that God's actions are good and beneficial; goodness is one of God's attributes—something that helps to define God. In fact, God is the source of *all* goodness. Jesus told the rich young ruler, "No one is good except God alone" (Luke 18:19), and James reminds us that "Every good gift and every perfect gift is from above, coming down from the Father of lights" (James 1:17).

So, no matter where you are or what you're going through, we want you to know that God is good. He loves you and delights in you, and His mercies are new every morning.

This first week we'll focus primarily on acknowledging God's goodness—both in terms of better understanding who He is and how to increase our awareness of the difference it makes in our lives.

The Origin of Goodness

**"Who has performed and done this,
calling the generations from the beginning?
I, the Lord, the first, and with the last; I am he."**

ISAIAH 41:4

WHEN WE'RE TALKING ABOUT GOD'S GOODNESS, where do we even begin? Some people love to go back to when they first encountered the wonderful goodness of God as they acknowledged what Jesus had done on their behalf and put their trust in Him. Others may recall a time when they were in dire straits, but a solution appeared out of nowhere, convincing them that it could only be God at work in their lives. Either way, it's a wonderful thing when the goodness of God ceases to be merely a cognitive belief and becomes a meaningful reality.

Yet we need to go back much, much further because God's goodness toward us existed long before we realized it. Scripture tells us that His goodness was first evidenced "in the beginning" when He created the world and human beings. But as we begin our look at God's goodness and mercy, we need to go back even further than that.

In one of Jesus' final prayers during His time on earth, He said that God loved Him "before the foundation of the world" (John 17:24). The Apostle Paul echoed that truth in some of his letters. Thanks to special revelation through Jesus, Paul was made privy to spiritual truths that otherwise would have likely remained a mystery to God's people. He explains: "For I would have you know, brothers, that the gospel that was preached by me is not man's gospel. For I did not receive it from any man, nor was I taught it, but I received it through a revelation of Jesus Christ" (Galatians 1:11-12).

As Paul begins his letter to the Ephesians, he informs his readers of God's preexistence—and why that should be significant to them. He speaks of God's love rather than goodness, but Megan and I believe the two are essentially the same. See for yourself:

> Blessed be the God and Father of our Lord Jesus Christ, who has blessed us in Christ with every spiritual blessing in the heavenly places, even as he chose us in him before the foundation of the world, that we should be holy and blameless before him. In love he predestined us for adoption to himself as sons through Jesus Christ, according to the purpose of his will, to the praise of his glorious grace, with which he has blessed us in the Beloved. (Ephesians 1:3-6)

Like many of Paul's theological explanations, he provides a lot for us to digest here, but let's take it in small bites to better comprehend what he's saying. If you are a believer, God was aware that you would be one of His before He even created the first human being! You have been blessed with "every spiritual blessing in the heavenly places." Wouldn't you consider that God's "goodness"? I know I do.

As hard as it is for human minds to comprehend, God has always existed. When we go back to *our* beginning—to the creation of the world—God was already there. He had no beginning. And since goodness is one of God's attributes, His goodness has also always existed. The world He created for humans to inhabit was "very good," and He started them off in a sinless state in direct communion with Him. He even had a plan of salvation long before He initiated life on earth, which we'll say more about later.

How are we to respond to God's unfathomable goodness toward us? Author Brennan Manning suggests: "We should be astonished at the goodness of God, stunned that He should bother to call us by name, our mouths wide open at His love, bewildered that at this very moment we are standing on holy ground."[1] That's a good start, at least! Our omniscient Lord knows everything about us (including the things we don't want anyone to know), and His love isn't diminished at all.

But one other question at this point . . . In the next study we will examine a few of the specific wonders of God's great creation. Before we get there, however, what would you say is the greatest of God's good creations?

When trying to describe the goodness and greatness of God in relatable terms, the psalmists and other Scripture writers often thought of mountains (Psalm 121:1-2), streams of fresh water (Psalm 42:1), and other symbols of life and strength. But in the New Testament, after Christ had brought salvation to the world and God had sent the Holy Spirit, Paul notes that we who have been saved by grace through faith are God's "workmanship, created in Christ Jesus for good works, which God prepared beforehand, that we should walk in them" (Ephesians 2:10).

The Greek word for *workmanship* is an artistic term that can also be interpreted as "masterpiece." And again, Paul affirms that God's handiwork was "prepared beforehand." In God's unsurpassable goodness, you were created as a magnificent work of art that He has had in mind since before His creation of Adam and Eve. As we've seen, God knows everything about us, including things we prefer to hide, but here, we realize that He sees us precious, valuable masterpieces! Hang on to that marvelous thought as you continue this study.

Reflect and Pray

1. When is the first time you can recall realizing and acknowledging the goodness of God?

2. Many people thank God for all He provides and does for us. But how often, if ever, do you pause to praise God specifically for His goodness (as you might for His attributes of holiness or power)? What do you think might be the benefits of doing so?

3. Reread Ephesians 1:3-6 a couple of times. List all the spiritual benefits you find there that are yours because of God's goodness "before the foundation of the world," and then note the significance of each one.

4. How do you feel when you do something nice for someone that goes unnoticed? Think back over the previous week. How many good gifts or experiences can you recall that either went unnoticed or that you took for granted? Remembering that everything good in life comes from God (James 1:17), what can you do to start being more appreciative of God's goodness in the future?

5. Ask God to open your eyes this week to make you more aware of the many good things He sends your way, and of the fact that you were created to do good works for others.

God's Goodness Is Seen in Creation

**How great is [God's] goodness,
and how great his beauty.**

ZECHARIAH 9:17

As we saw in the previous study, God's goodness has always existed. While most of us find it difficult (if not impossible!) to wrap our heads around that fact, it's a bit more practical to consider how His goodness has influenced our lives up till now. God loves and cares for all people, regardless of income, education, or physical ability. He also surrounds us with beauty, although, as you may have heard, beauty is often in the eye of the beholder.

Some of us have a Goldilocks attitude about the definition of *beautiful*. In reference to a beautiful day, if the temperature varies more than a couple of degrees from 72°, it's either too hot or too cold for them. If the sun's not shining, they complain about the gloom. After God blesses them with a refreshing shower, they complain, "I was hoping for a pretty day." But then, if they get too many sunny days without rain, they worry about drought and the condition of their gardens.

Yet thanks to mass communications and social media, recent generations have witnessed the vast diversity of beauty across the earth in previously unavailable (or even unseen) locations—including some of the hottest and coldest, wettest and driest places. In response, many people invest great time and expense to plan vacations that enable them to see firsthand the wonders of nature that former generations never knew existed. You can retreat to a tropical island for snorkeling or scuba to see the beauty beneath the water, go north to ski during the day and then stay at an ice hotel, take an African photo safari, or consider thousands of other options to personally witness more of God's phenomenal creation.

But let's not miss the beauty of God's good creation wherever we are. The National Park Service has preserved special places across the country for people to visit, but you need even go that far. My husband Tim loves to take drives out in the country, and we often go to a favorite spot where I can both see and feel God's goodness all around me. The location has beautiful views of the mountains, highlighted in color during the early evenings with the sunset approaching. When we take our granddaughters with us, we love to watch them fish, wade through the creek, and catch butterflies and fireflies. It's truly a beautiful place—and not far from where we live and work. Even when I'm beset by long days and busy weeks, and can't get away physically, I can pause for a moment to remember God's goodness and beauty in that place. It's my way to observe Psalm 46:10: "Be still, and know that I am God." And when I do, I find I'm better able to see God's goodness right where I am, among my also-busy coworkers, my always-busy family, and everywhere I look.

As we work with women, Megan and I have found that many feel connected to God through His creation. Think about your own experience of being out in nature and feeling a special closeness to God. Were you at a beach? In the mountains? At a remote cabin surrounded by woods? Beside a roaring waterfall? Maybe in your own home garden with your hands in the soil and the sun on your face?

Many of us are regularly reminded of God's goodness because we bring nature into our homes and everyday lives in the form of pets—furry friends who reward us with unconditional love. Others are blessed to see God's goodness every day at their worksite. Megan, for example, works in the medical field and often speaks in awe of the intricacies of the human body.

Scripture tells us that we can learn what God is like (His attributes) through creation. To begin with, we see that God is personally involved with His creation:

> Who has measured the waters in the hollow of his hand and marked off the heavens with a span, enclosed the dust of the earth in a measure and weighed the mountains in scales and the hills in a balance? Who has measured the Spirit of the Lord, or what man shows him his counsel? Whom did he consult, and who made him understand?

Who taught him the path of justice, and taught him knowledge, and showed him the way of understanding? Behold, the nations are like a drop from a bucket, and are accounted as the dust on the scales; behold, he takes up the coastlands like fine dust. (Isaiah 40:12-15)

And God's creation isn't limited to the great diversity of plants, animals, and landscapes we enjoy here on earth. It includes the stars, planets, and galaxies, going even beyond the hundreds of billions of celestial spheres we can see with our most advanced telescopes. And each one is special to Him:

Lift up your eyes on high and see: who created these? He who brings out their host by number, calling them all by name; by the greatness of his might and because he is strong in power, not one is missing. (Isaiah 40:26)

God's goodness is evident through the creation story. Every now and then, we need to stop and smell the roses—literally. Don't let yourself get into the habit of overlooking all the beauty and goodness around you.

Reflect and Pray

1. In what ways do you see God's goodness in His physical creation? Where in nature are you most likely to feel closest to Him?

2. Review Isaiah 40:12-15. How do these examples help you better understand the scope of God's involvement in nature?

3. What are some first steps you can take to intentionally attempt to connect with God more effectively?

4. Reread Psalm 46:10. We know what it means to "be still," but what do you think it means to "know that God is God"?

5. Spend some time today outside (or looking out a window). Note everything you see that is part of God's good creation. Thank Him for each one.

God's Goodness Is Experienced in Relationships

The Lord God said, "It is not good that the man should be alone; I will make him a helper fit for him."

GENESIS 2:18

LAST YEAR MY WHOLE FAMILY took an Alaskan cruise with the American Association of Christian Counselors (AACC), and it has become one of my favorite special memories. Many of our family members are involved with AACC at different levels, so this was a work trip that involved much prayerful planning. Still, God's hand moved on the trip, and we made plenty of time to connect with our friends and colleagues. (Those who have been to our EWomen conferences have heard us say that as busy as we are, we love to center our lives around time with family, and we make sure to balance work time with fun and connecting experiences.)

We also took time to get into nature and reflect on the beauty of God's creation with our family. As the ship moved through glaciers, we admired the white-capped peaks and the calm blue ice all around us. In the morning, before the workshops and worship sessions began, we enjoyed hot chocolate on our balcony, taking in the incredible scenery and amazing wildlife. Whales and dolphins swam alongside the ship, and seals watched us from nearby ice. We even saw grizzly bears and deer in the distance while eagles soared above. Seeing the joy and wonder on Olivia's and Sophia's faces (5 and 2 at the time) was more special than watching all the animals! There's something remarkable about seeing the world through a child's eyes, and childlike wonder is such an appropriate response to God's handiwork.

Yesterday's study called attention to the variety of nature and the goodness inherent in all of God's creation. Yet we don't get very far through Genesis before we find something that's *not* good, as you can see in the today's passage. Adam had an enviable relationship with God, who had formed him from the dust of the earth and breathed into his nostrils the breath of life. God had planted a garden for Adam to care for that was filled with all kinds of trees that were both "pleasant to the sight and good for food"—and with one critical exception, Adam was free to eat at will from any of the trees. God had also given Adam the privilege of naming the livestock, birds, and other beasts. Yet as good as the relationship was between God and Adam, the Lord knew Adam needed something (someone) else, so He created woman (Genesis 2:5-25).

Adam (and later Eve) had a close personal relationship with his Creator like no one has had since, and yet God realized he needed more. As Adam named the animals and no doubt saw them in pairs, he must have also realized that something was lacking in his life. I think there's a lesson here for all of us: As wonderful as it is to personally experience God's magnificent goodness and abundant provision, it's even better to experience it among a group of fellow believers.

Noted psychiatrist John Bowlby said that intimate attachments to other human beings are the hub around which a person's life revolves.[2] I suspect Adam might have agreed—without necessarily diminishing his relationship with God. Perhaps that's why Jesus, when challenged to identify the most important commandment, said, "You shall love the Lord your God with all your heart and with all your soul and with all your mind. This is the great and first commandment . . ." But He didn't stop there. He immediately added, "And a second is like it: You shall love your neighbor as yourself. On these two commandments depend all the Law and the Prophets" (Matthew 22:37-40). Jesus' disciple John later realized that it was impossible to have a proper loving relationship with God if it didn't include love for one another as well: "He who does not love his brother whom he has seen cannot love God whom he has not seen" (1 John 4:20).

God's goodness is to be experienced personally, and then it is meant to be shared with others. In Colossians 2:6-7, we read about the importance of our relationship with Christ: "Therefore, as you received Christ Jesus the Lord, so walk in him, rooted and built up in him and established in the faith, just as you were taught, abounding in thanksgiving."

When I think about being "rooted" in Christ, it calls to mind the image of a tree deeply planted in rich soil, drawing nourishment from its source. Jesus used a similar image to describe His relationship with His disciples: "I am the vine; you are the branches.

Whoever abides in me and I in him, he it is that bears much fruit, for apart from me you can do nothing" (John 15:5).

As long as our relationship with Christ remains strong, God's goodness continues to flow into our lives. And the "fruit" that we bear includes the relationships we form with others that enable them to receive that same abundant goodness. We'll look more at goodness and bearing fruit in the next study.

Reflect and Pray

1. Recall a time or two when your sense of joy and gratitude for God's goodness was intensified when you were among a group. What makes those experiences so memorable?

2. Did you notice that God didn't wait for Adam to complain about loneliness before providing him with a mate? Do you think this is significant? Explain your answer.

3. Read I John 4:7-21. Do you think it's possible to love God without loving other people? Do you think it's possible to love other people without loving God? Explain.

4. Review Colossians 2:6-7. How securely are you "rooted" in your relationship with Christ? What might you do to make that relationship even stronger?

5. Spend time thanking God for good friends and family members who have made His goodness more evident to you throughout your lifetime.

Finding Our Purpose in God's Design

We always pray for you, that our God may make you worthy of his calling and may fulfill every resolve for good and every work of faith by his power.

2 THESSALONIANS 1:11

YESTERDAY WE SAW GOD'S GOODNESS extended to Adam through the creation of a woman to be his companion. We also saw that God had given Adam work to do—tending to the garden of Eden and naming the animals (Genesis 2:15, 19-20). Some people tend to have a knee-jerk reaction to associating God's goodness with the necessity of working. They may not say it aloud, but they think, *If God is good, why do I need to slave every day at a job I can't stand and that doesn't pay nearly enough?*

However, we see that work was part of God's good plan for humanity from the beginning. Science and personal experience seem to agree. Pastor Tim Keller wrote, "Work is as much a basic human need as food, beauty, rest, friendship, prayer, and sexuality; it is not simply medicine but food for our soul. Without meaningful work, we sense significant inner loss and emptiness."[3]

I find it humbling to think that God entrusted Adam and Eve with the task of stewarding the garden, not because He needed their help, but because He wanted them to experience the joy and fulfillment of working alongside Him. Today, we still carry that calling to care for God's creation, but even more so, we are invited to reflect on what it reveals about His character. We discover that finding a productive area of service to God and others is indeed another source of God's goodness.

As I watch my granddaughters grow up, I see them already dreaming of fulfilling a significant purpose. Every day, Sophia pulls out her little doctor's kit and gets to work. She loves being a doctor, just like her mommy, and she takes her job very seriously. She checks my heart and insists on giving me four shots, whether I want them or not. Poor Bubba, our dog, gets the same treatment. My daily prayer is that she remembers to put the thermometer in my mouth before Bubba's!

My older granddaughter, Olivia, is just as imaginative as Sophia, though her interests lean a little differently. At five, she loves pretending to be a dermatologist. She'll look at moles and confidently give us a correct identification using the medical terms she's picked up. She also loves to play schoolteacher, especially imitating her beloved teacher, Mrs. Drake. Watching her eagerness to learn and play is such a joy.

I see God's goodness in the innate purpose He has built inside of us. We looked at Ephesians 2:10 on Day 1 this week to discover that humans are God's masterpiece, but the verse also reminds us that we were created with a purpose in mind: "For we are his workmanship, created in Christ Jesus for good works, which God prepared beforehand, that we should walk in them."

Paul builds on this idea by showing us how God equips us uniquely for His purposes:

> For as in one body we have many members, and the members do not all have the same function, so we, though many, are one body in Christ, and individually members one of another. Having gifts that differ according to the grace given to us, let us use them: if prophecy, in proportion to our faith; if service, in our serving; the one who teaches, in his teaching; the one who exhorts, in his exhortation; the one who contributes, in generosity; the one who leads, with zeal; the one who does acts of mercy, with cheerfulness. (Romans 12:4-8)

I love how practical this passage is, showing that no gift is too small or unimportant in God's kingdom. Every ability and talent is given intentionally, and we are called to use them all faithfully wherever God has placed us. Whether we are leading a team, encouraging a friend, or simply serving in small ways that go unnoticed by others, our faithfulness contributes to His greater plan. God has equipped us with exactly what we need to make an impact for His glory, which also provides personal satisfaction and contentment.

How does this relate to God's goodness? Today's opening Scripture from 2 Thessalonians 1:11 shows that God's calling enables and empowers us to extend his goodness to others. Our Creator didn't have to make us all so unique or give us the desire and ability to pursue such varied passions. Just think how different your life would be if God had created only one kind of food, only the animals needed for human survival, only one personality among human beings. Wouldn't that be a terribly monotonous (dare I say *boring*?) way to live?

Your individuality is a gift. Don't waste time and energy wishing you were someone else. Determine what your unique gifts are and use them for God's kingdom. When you discover God's plan for you, your life takes on new purpose.

Reflect and Pray

1. Are any of your current interests and abilities the result of childhood ambitions? In what ways?

2. Review Romans 12:4-8. What are your spiritual gifts? How can identifying your God-given gifts help you realize God's goodness?

3. Reflect on a recent experience where you used your gifts to help others. How did it impact your faith?

4. How does understanding that you have a unique purpose help you feel more connected to God?

5. If you've never tried to identify your spiritual gifts, spend some time trying to determine what they are. (Begin with Romans 12:1-8; 1 Corinthians 12; Ephesians 4:11-16; and 1 Peter 4:7-11. Numerous other resources are also available.) Then, consider how to apply those gifts as you clarify God's plan for you and begin to live with a greater sense of purpose.

DAY 5

God's Goodness Prompts Other Blessings

Lift up your eyes on high and see: who created these? He who brings out their host by number, calling them all by name; by the greatness of his might and because he is strong in power, not one is missing.

ISAIAH 40:26

MOST OF MY FAMILY LIVE NEAR OUR ALMA MATER, Liberty University (LU), where you will find the LU Astronomical Observatory. To minimize light pollution, the observatory was built in a huge field in a rural, remote area away from the school. The closest neighbors are the horses at the equestrian center. Anyone in the community can come on clear nights to view the planets, moon, and stars through one of the biggest and most advanced engineering telescopes in the region. Helpful guides explain which constellations are more visible at different times of the year and share facts about the stars that point back to our loving Creator. For example, with an estimated 100 billion stars or more just in the Milky Way, imagine the Lord having a name for each and every star. And from there, the universe just goes on and on, seemingly endlessly.

As we wind up this week's study with its focus on God's goodness in creation, I want to put one more exclamation point on the *extent* of His goodness. The God who created the stars and knows each one by name also knows when a sparrow falls on earth. He knows the number of hairs on your head (Matthew 10:29-30). He knows every human being personally and intimately. As there is no limit on the extent of the universe, neither is there any limit to God's goodness shown to His people.

Many of God's other attributes flow out of or in conjunction with His incredible goodness. As we begin to comprehend, acknowledge, and apply God's goodness in our everyday lives, we too see other positive results. Here's how the Apostle Paul explained it to his associate, Titus:

> When the goodness and loving kindness of God our Savior appeared, he saved us, not because of works done by us in righteousness, but according to his own mercy, by the washing of regeneration and renewal of the Holy Spirit, whom he poured out on us richly through Jesus Christ our Savior, so that being justified by his grace we might become heirs according to the hope of eternal life. The saying is trustworthy, and I want you to insist on these things, so that those who have believed in God may be careful to devote themselves to good works. These things are excellent and profitable for people. (Titus 3:4-8)

Notice what began to happen "when the goodness and loving kindness of God our Savior appeared": salvation; mercy (which will be our focus next week); regeneration and renewal brought by the pouring out of the Holy Spirit; grace that enables us to stand before God, justified; and the confidence that we will inherit all God has promised us as we look forward to eternal life. How are we to respond to all these benefits that derive from the goodness of God? We devote ourselves to goodness in our relationships with others.

Before we can effectively help someone else through difficulty, we must experience God's goodness personally. I've talked and prayed with many women who struggle to experience the many benefits of God's loving goodness because parents or other overseers failed to affirm their value and worth. Connecting with God's love is usually difficult for those hindered by previous failures or disappointments. It may feel emotionally traumatic or even overwhelming to address those feelings, but please don't go another day without asking God to help you experience His amazing love for you. Consider spending more time with the Lord in nature, in worship, or reading His Word. If past sins feel like a hindrance, you can be sure that He will forgive you, although you may need to work on forgiving yourself. It can help to seek out a wise and trustworthy older woman to mentor you through this.

And then, the next time you're outside at night and the stars are out, remember that God knows the name of each one. Pastor Louie Giglio has said, "God calls each and every star by name. It's not likely He has forgotten yours." Think about how, beyond those stars, the universe just keeps going on and on and on. And then remind yourself that God's goodness is just as vast and endless as the universe. This world can be a difficult, lonely, and scary place, but Scripture assures us that we are not alone, unnoticed, or insignificant. God created you uniquely and individually. He knows you by name and personally values you . . . and with time, so will other people. Don't give up on God's goodness, because He never gives up on you.

Also, keep reading because next week's focus on God's mercy should encourage all of us, but especially those struggling with self-criticism or forgiveness issues.

Reflect and Pray

1. Now that you've spent a week thinking about God's goodness, have you learned anything you didn't already know?

2. When you see that God knows the name of every star, sees the death of every sparrow, and knows everything about you (including the number of hairs on your head), how does it make you feel to realize He is so intimately involved in each of His creations?

3. Have you ever struggled to feel worthy in God's eyes? How might nature help you be surer of His love and goodness for you?

4. Review Titus 3:4-8 and all the benefits that accompany God's goodness. Have you personally experienced each one? What other benefits can you think of?

5. Wherever you are in your spiritual growth journey, as you begin to better comprehend all that God is doing for you, what are some steps you can take to show your gratitude by helping others understand and realize His goodness?

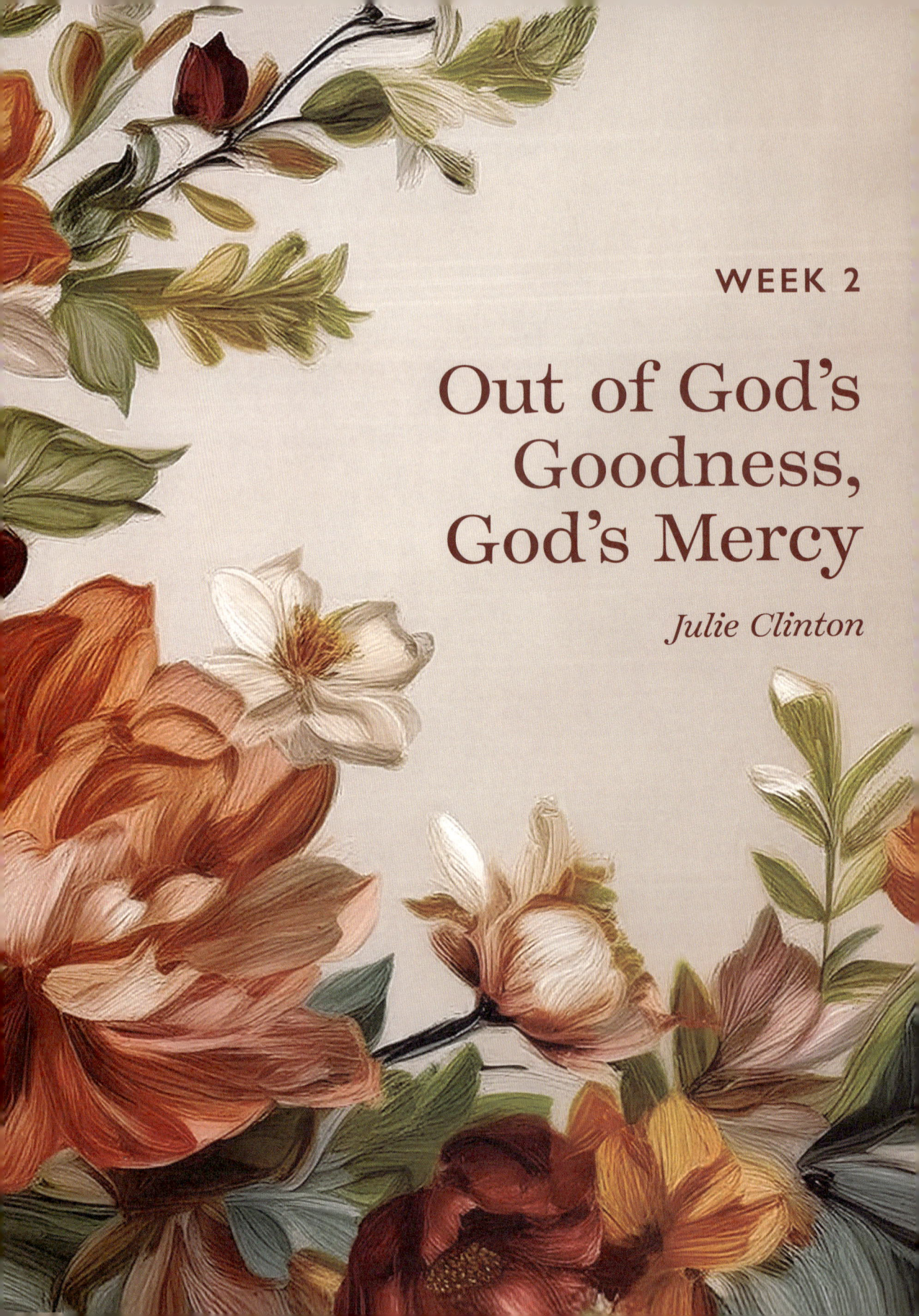

Out of God's Goodness, God's Mercy

Julie Clinton

My grandparents were German North American church planters in Calgary, Canada. We called my grandmother Oma, and my grandfather was Opa. Early in their ministry they were filling in at a church that was awaiting the arrival of a new pastor. During that time, a nearby hospital had arranged to take on babies that new mothers in that area couldn't care for. Desiring to connect the motherless babies to loving homes, the hospital invited clergy members to adopt the infants and waived all fees involved.

My grandparents felt a tug on their hearts to visit the hospital. On their first visit, Oma and Opa adopted a little girl they named Murna. Two years later, on May 13, 1940, they returned to the same hospital with every intention of adopting a baby boy. Oma waited in the hallway as Opa went into the nursery to meet their new son. A few minutes later, he walked out, cradling a baby girl in his arms.

My Oma, a bit surprised, said, "I thought you were going to choose a boy!"

My Opa, as a young husband and father, looked down at the little girl nestled against him and replied, "This little one looked up at me, and her eyes met mine." That moment of connection, just a glance, was enough for them to know she was meant to be theirs.

That little girl grew up to be my mother. My mom's story is a beautiful reminder to me of God's mercy at work. Just as my grandparents saw her need and chose to bring her into their family, God, in His mercy, sees each of us in our moments of vulnerability. Even after we've ignored or defied Him, He doesn't leave us alone or abandoned; instead, He reaches out and offers us a place in His family. My mother's adoption reminds me that God's mercy isn't just an abstract concept—it's active, tangible, and life-changing.

Like God's goodness, His mercy is abundant and ongoing. My mother led a long and faithful life, but in her later years she suffered greatly from scleroderma and a stroke that took away her ability to recognize family members. On my days with her, I would take a devotional, and as I read, all the nursing assistants would come in and listen too. Those moments became a precious time of sharing God's goodness. I would ask Mom if she wanted to pray, but she would shake her head and point to me, so I'd pray, and then we'd sing together. Amazingly, even though she couldn't say my name, she could still sing every word of those old hymns, pronouncing every line clearly and harmonizing with perfect alto.

Seeing her remember those hymns encouraged me with the realization that the truths God plants in our hearts never fade. As a little girl, my mother was redeemed from a place of abandonment and brought into a home where she learned that Jesus died for her. Her last days were filled with memories of God's goodness, and every hymn was a reminder of the faith she'd held her whole life.

Last week we focused on God's goodness as we recounted His creation of a beautiful and perfect world. But we now live in a far-from-perfect world, so what happens when God is good but we aren't? This week our focus will be on God's mercy, which grows out of His steadfast goodness.

One of the theological books in my husband's library defines mercy as "that aspect of God's goodness that causes God to show pity and compassion."[4] A perfect world doesn't need God's mercy, but ours surely does. We need God's mercy after we sin against Him or other people. But we also need His mercy when the circumstances of life create physical pain and emotional distress in our lives. Watching my mother's struggles late in life taught me to lean into God's compassion, even during seasons of discomfort and uncertainty.

Whether we're navigating personal struggles, walking alongside loved ones in their pain, or facing fears about the future, we always depend on God's goodness and mercy (Deuteronomy 31:6). He is with us, and His work in our lives is unshakable. Let's take time this week to reflect on the ways His goodness and mercy have carried us through difficult situations and proven that His presence is a constant source of strength.

The First Act of Mercy

**Let us then with confidence draw near to the throne of grace,
that we may receive mercy
and find grace to help in time of need.**

HEBREWS 4:16

I HOPE LAST WEEK'S STUDIES opened your eyes to the extent and influence of God's goodness in our world. Many of the examples came from the book of Genesis, specifically the Creation story. Before moving on, I'd like to spend one more day in that time frame to demonstrate how God's goodness is connected to His mercy.

We saw that when God placed Adam in the garden of Eden as a caretaker, Adam was given the privilege of eating from any of the trees . . . except one. And God's warning to avoid eating from that tree was explicit: "You may surely eat of every tree of the garden, but of the tree of the knowledge of good and evil you shall not eat, for in the day that you eat of it you shall surely die" (Genesis 2:16-17).

I'm sure you know the story. One day the serpent showed up and used lies and half-truths to entice Eve to eat the forbidden fruit. She shared it with Adam, who ate willingly. Immediately, "the eyes of both were opened," they realized they were naked, and they fashioned some clothing made from fig leaves. Then, rather than coming out to meet with God as usual, they hid from Him. When God finally confronted them, they both tried to shift the blame for their blatant disobedience (Genesis 3:1-13).

God was displeased, for good reason, and He imposed penalties on all three involved: the serpent, Adam, and Eve. In addition, Adam and Eve were removed from the garden because God didn't want them to eat from the tree of life and live forever with no atonement for their sin (Genesis 3:14-24).

Still, after those events we see God's goodness and mercy at work. To replace their hastily made fig-leaf wardrobe, God provided clothing made of animal skins—the first indication of death in God's new creation (Genesis 3:21). And although God had warned that disobedience would lead to death, which it eventually did, Adam and Eve didn't die immediately. Adam first lived to the impressive age of 930 and had other sons and daughters after Cain and Abel (Genesis 5:3-5). In His mercy, God didn't bring humanity to an end because of the sin of earth's first inhabitants, and He doesn't give up on any of us when we too ignore or defy His clear instructions.

We spoke only of God's goodness in last week's sessions because there was no need for mercy in a world not yet affected by sin. But as soon as Adam and Eve disregarded God's will and fulfilled their own desires instead, God's mercy quickly became evident. Oh, they still had to suffer the consequences of their sin. From that point forward, Adam and his descendants had to make a living "by the sweat of [their] face" as they battled "thorns and thistles" to get food. Eve and her descendants would have pain in childbearing—which makes me wonder if she'd had children without pain. (Cain's wife had to come from somewhere [Genesis 4:17].)

But the biggest act of mercy in this account is found in the curse imposed on the serpent. God said, "I will put enmity between you and the woman, and between your offspring and her offspring; he shall bruise your head, and you shall bruise his heel" (Genesis 3:15). Most theologians concur that this is the earliest prophecy of a coming Messiah/savior for God's people. The serpent's offspring (those who intentionally practice evil) will strike a blow against the woman's offspring (Jesus), but her offspring would have the ultimate victory.

We should never give up on God because He never gives up on us. If we believe He has deserted us, we need to think again. See what God says through Isaiah:

> Sing for joy, O heavens, and exult, O earth; break forth, O mountains, into singing! For the Lord has comforted his people and will have compassion on his afflicted. But Zion said, "The Lord has forsaken me; my Lord has forgotten me." Can a woman forget her nursing child, that she should have no compassion on the son of her womb? Even these may forget, yet I will not forget you. Behold, I have engraved you on the palms of my hands; your walls are continually before me. (Isaiah 49:13-16)

God is more committed to you than a mother is to the children she gives birth to. Many times, we are much harder on ourselves than God would ever be toward us. When we've done something that has resulted in feelings of guilt and shame, we don't even want to admit it to ourselves—much less confess it to God or someone else. But God is merciful and quick to forgive.

When you find yourself in need of God's forgiveness (which for most of us is quite often), remember that God is merciful. Rather than hiding from God, which was Adam's instinct, help is found by drawing *nearer* to God. Reread the passage from Hebrews that opens today's study. God is the source of goodness and mercy, so the sooner we make things right with Him through confession, the sooner we receive His mercy and realize our guilt has been removed.

Never doubt the extent and availability of God's mercy. Charles Spurgeon wrote, "God's mercy is so great that you may sooner drain the sea of its water, or deprive the sun of its light, or make space too narrow, than diminish the great mercy of God."[5] It's a wonderful comfort to discover that no matter what goes wrong in your life, or what *you* do wrong, God's mercy provides forgiveness, strength, and a renewed relationship with Him.

Reflect and Pray

1. What do you think of God's response to Adam's and Eve's disobedience? Do you think it was too harsh? Did they get off too easy? Or do you think it was appropriate?

2. Before God could show mercy by improving Adam's and Eve's clothing, animals had to die. What was the cost of God's ability to forgive our sins and mercifully restore us to His good favor?

3. Review Isaiah 49:13-16. How do you respond to the fact that God never forgets or forsakes you"?

4. Hebrews 4:16 encourages us to confidently draw near to God and expect to receive His mercy and grace. Do you believe that, or have you maybe had a different image of God in the past? Explain.

5. With this fresh review of God's mercy, take time this week to find a private spot and spend a time of confession for anything that might be on your mind.

Mercy During Brokenness

We are afflicted in every way, but not crushed; perplexed, but not driven to despair; persecuted, but not forsaken; struck down, but not destroyed.

2 CORINTHIANS 4:8-9

HAVE YOU EVER FELT BROKEN? When Megan and I wrote *Women Following Jesus*, I talked about following the ambulance that took my dad home after finally losing his battle with cancer. I thought to myself, *This is the last time that I will follow my dad somewhere*. That was one of the most broken experiences of my life. We all have those broken times—some are moments, others are seasons. The difficulty often stems from illness, dissolved relationships, or loss. Sometimes the circumstances take us by complete surprise and hurt in a way for which we are completely unprepared.

Thankfully, Scripture offers good news for our times of brokenness, and the answer is again found in God's mercy and goodness. The Bible tells us over and over about these attributes of God. Jesus reminds us to "Be merciful, even as your Father is merciful" (Luke 6:36). Even more encouraging is that God never runs out of mercy. Ephesians 2:4 explains that because of God's great love He is "rich in mercy." That's a good thing for us humans who are "rich" in problems that require a compassionate Savior! Whether we turn to the Lord in brokenness, humility, sorrow, grief, or fear, He responds with healing mercy that never runs out.

Sometimes brokenness comes from regret over past sins. If you are part of the EWomen+ membership, perhaps you've heard our friend, Dr. Megan Clunan, talk about overcoming shame. She shares how the Lord wants us to feel repentance, which draws us closer to Him, yet He never expects us to suffer stagnantly in regret and shame. She says, "God does not reveal shortcomings to us; simply leave us in those spaces and allow us to be defined by them. He came to reveal our shortcomings to us so that we are not prey to them any longer, but are able to be called into repentance." (If you would like to hear Dr. Megan's full talk on overcoming shame, it is one of many videos available in our EWomen+ membership.)

Repentance means to come back to our heavenly Father and be reunited with Him, but many people confuse repentance with regret. A comparison between the two is made in 2 Corinthians 7:9-10: " I rejoice, not because you were grieved, but because you were grieved into repenting. For you felt a godly grief, so that you suffered no loss through us. For godly grief produces a repentance that leads to salvation without regret, whereas worldly grief produces death."

If your brokenness makes you feel deeper shame and grief, you're probably feeling regret and are unable to do anything that makes you feel better. But if you replace that regret with repentance and leave yourself at God's mercy, that's exactly what you'll get—His gentle mercy and love.

When David had his affair with Bathsheba and she became pregnant, David compounded his sin by arranging to have her husband Uriah killed in battle. Later, God sent a prophet named Nathan to confront him with the message that the child of his union with Bathsheba would die. When the child became sick, David fasted and prayed for seven days, hoping the child would live. But when the boy died, David cleaned himself up and began to worship God. His servants didn't understand his behavior, but David explained that he had had left the matter in God's hands. He wrote Psalm 51 in response, in which he confessed to God, "I know my transgressions, and my sin is ever before me. Against you, you only, have I sinned and done evil in your sight" (Psalm 51:3-4). David's sin was grievous, but his repentance was sincere. In God's mercy, the next child David and Bathsheba had was Solomon, who was chosen above all his other children to be the next king of Israel (2 Samuel 12).

Later sessions will say more about how Jesus knows our struggles. Today, however, I'd like us to remember that God's mercy is gentle and compassionate, offering hope and restoration to all who feel broken. We can turn to Him when we are hurt by others and the sinfulness in this broken world—illness, death, mistreatment, and other sufferings. And because God's mercy is so great, we are just as welcome to turn to Him even when our pain is caused by our own missteps and mistakes. God's mercy doesn't condemn, but lifts us up with compassion.

Reflect and Pray

1. Have you ever felt broken and wallowed in regret for a long period? Is the problem still lingering? If not, how was it resolved?

2. Review 2 Corinthians 7:9-10, and then explain in your own words the difference between regret and repentance. How does mercy make a difference when you're trying to get past a personal failure or are overwhelmed by other problems?

3. What does it mean to you that God is "rich in mercy"?

4. How can you extend God's gentle mercy to others when conflicts arise in your personal relationships?

5. Try to recall an example or two when God's mercy enabled you to be "afflicted in every way, but not crushed; perplexed, but not driven to despair; persecuted, but not forsaken; or struck down, but not destroyed." Thank God for those times and then pray for a growing and more consistent awareness of God's great mercy in your daily routines.

DAY 3

A New Thing

**"Remember not the former things, nor consider
the things of old. Behold, I am doing a new thing;
now it springs forth, do you not perceive it?
I will make a way in the wilderness and rivers in the desert."**

ISAIAH 43:18-19

GOD'S MERCY BRINGS NEW BEGINNINGS, which often result in impressive and incredible changes. We see this in nature with the changing seasons. Spring, summer, and fall all offer beauty and color. And while winter has a beauty of its own, the landscape becomes much more bleak, bare, and cold—at least, in my part of the world. I still get excited by a beautiful snowfall, yet I'm always ready for spring. Every spring is "a new thing." Trees and flowers bud out again, birds resume their morning singing, neighbors linger outside long enough for conversations, and the increased warmth of the sun seems to go straight to our hearts and spirits.

Our lives go through similar seasons. Some periods are like carefree summer days without a concern in the world, and others are wintry cold and harsh. We can look to nature to remind us that creation continues moving forward and see that even in difficult seasons, God creates clear paths and streams of hope. He offers us a fresh start, the chance to let go of past mistakes, and the opportunity to embrace new opportunities He provides.

Scripture is very clear that your past does not define your future. Although we all may feel guilty for previous mistakes or intentional sins, if you are stuck in guilt and shame, that is not from God. He always offers mercy, forgiveness, and a fresh start. Author Anne Lamott reminds us:

Mercy is radical kindness. Mercy means offering or being offered aid in desperate straits. Mercy is not deserved. It involves absolving the unabsolvable, forgiving the unforgiveable. Mercy brings us to the miracle of apology, given and accepted, to unashamed humility when we have erred or forgotten. Charge it to our heads and not our hearts, as the elders in black churches have long said.[6]

Believers today rely on God's mercy as a country, as a church, and as individuals. We base our confidence in His merciful forgiveness on numerous stories throughout Scripture. Let's look at just a few examples:

» After the great flood, God gave humanity a fresh start on the earth with faithful Noah, using a rainbow as a reminder of His promise to never again cover the earth in a flood (Genesis 6-9).

» Ruth's story began with heartache—widowed and trying to make a living for herself and her mother-in-law, Naomi, in a foreign land. On their own, the two women faced an uncertain future. Yet because of Ruth's faithfulness and loyalty to Naomi and to God, her story didn't end in despair. God gave her a new beginning, a new family, and a new purpose through her marriage to Boaz, setting her on a path that would ultimately place her in the lineage of Christ (Ruth 1-4).

» Peter was left weeping with the sting of regret after denying Jesus three times on the night of His arrest (Matthew 26:69-75). Can you imagine the shame and heartache he must have felt? Yet after Jesus' resurrection, an angel sent word especially to Peter (Mark 16:6-7), and later Jesus renewed Peter's calling to serve (John 21:15-19).

» Saul was a devoted Pharisee who zealously persecuted Christians before being stopped in his tracks on the road to Damascus by a divine encounter with Jesus himself. His fresh start not only included a new name, Paul, but also a new mission: to spread the gospel he had once fought to suppress (Acts 9:1-30).

These stories and many others remind us that God's mercy is not just about wiping the slate clean—it's about providing His forgiven people with new hope, redemption, and promise. When we think about the new chapters God writes for our lives, we see His hand guiding us toward growth and purpose, even after seasons of heartache or failure. His mercy isn't passive; it's active, shaping us into who He created us to be. Just as Ruth stepped into a new family and a significant role in God's plan, and Peter was restored to lead and encourage the early church, God's mercy doesn't leave us where we are. It transforms us, equips us, and sends us forward. His mercy reminds us that we're never defined by our past mistakes or circumstances, but by the love and grace He pours out on us every day. Moving forward in His mercy means embracing the new thing He's doing and trusting that His plans for us are always good, even when they take us down unexpected paths.

Reflect and Pray

1. This session contained only a few of the many examples of God's abundant mercy recorded in the Bible. What are some others you can think of that are meaningful to you?

2. Reread Isaiah 43:18-19. What "new thing(s)" would you like to see God do for you?

3. What "former things" might you need to leave behind to allow you to boldly move forward into His new purpose for your life?

4. Do you think you've ever missed out on something new God was willing to do for you because you were holding out for something *you* wanted? Give an example.

5. Eventually, Jesus promises to make "all things new" (Revelation 21:5), but why wait? Pray that God will regularly show you new insights and opportunities in your spiritual walk with Him—and that you would respond to each new beginning that He mercifully offers.

The God of Compassion

**The steadfast love of the Lord never ceases;
his mercies never come to an end; they are new every
morning; great is your faithfulness.**

LAMENTATIONS 3:22-23

So far, we've looked at God's mercy in terms of His response to our personal shortcomings, which seems appropriate because that seems to be the clearest picture of mercy for many of us. We know what we've done wrong, we feel terrible about it, and only God is able to forgive the offense and give us a fresh start.

But Scripture uses the term in another sense. In the introduction to this week's devotions, I said that mercy has been defined as "that aspect of God's goodness that causes God to show pity and compassion." That's certain true when we've sinned against God in some way, but it's also true of God's nature in general.

Occasionally, as in the case of the Lamentations passage above, Scripture refers to God's *mercies*—plural. In such instances, it indicates the merciful actions of God. Essentially the mercies of God equate to God's *compassion*.

The more time I spend in ministry, the more I see how many women come to conferences with a pressing need for love and compassion. I see so many people walking around deeply hurting, but rather than finding compassion, they continue to experience more and greater hurt inflicted by other hurting people.

Sometimes, walking around in this broken world can make it easy to lose sight of God's goodness. Lately we're witnessing so much anger simmering just beneath the surface— road rage on the highways, angry customers lashing out at helpless cashiers in stores, and not even a modicum of grace when it comes to political opinions. It's heartbreaking to see how common it has become for people to lead with anger with no attempt to display understanding or empathy. But when I take a step back, I remind myself that so much of this anger often comes from a deeper place of fear or hurt. People carry heavy burdens, and sometimes that pain spills out in ways that damage others. The pain doesn't excuse the behavior, but it helps me to remember that this world is filled with people who are struggling—people who desperately need to experience the mercy and goodness of God.

I think we could all agree that we would like to have a more compassionate world, yet it's hard to practice something you've never experienced. For those who don't know, have never been told about, or feel as if they've been denied God's compassion, there is no peace. But those who know God discover they can feel peace even in turbulent circumstances:

> "Though the mountains be shaken and the hills be removed, yet my unfailing love for you will not be shaken nor my covenant of peace be removed," says the Lord, who has compassion on you. (Isaiah 54:10, NIV)

The peace that matters is God's covenant of peace with us. That peace and His unfailing love are present even when the mountains are shaking and the hills are moved. Notice that Scripture doesn't say, "because God has compassion, the mountains will never shake." No. Even when the mountains are trembling and your footing seems unsure, God's compassion and love remain steady. His love is unfailing and His peace unshakable, even when life feels like it's crumbling around us.

This truth has been such a comfort to me, especially during times of uncertainty or fear. God's love is not conditional or fleeting—it's steadfast, enduring, and rooted in His very nature. When we lean into His compassion, we experience a peace that calms our hearts, strengthens our faith, and allows us to extend that same compassion to others. It's a peace that goes beyond human understanding, and one that enables us to be compassionate with others. Author Henri Nouwen explains:

> When we honestly ask ourselves which person in our lives means the most to us, we often find that it is those who, instead of giving advice, solutions, or cures, have chosen rather to share our pain and touch our wounds with a warm and tender hand. The friend who

can be silent with us in a moment of despair or confusion, who can stay with us in an hour of grief and bereavement, who can tolerate not-knowing, not-curing, not-healing and face with us the reality of our powerlessness, that is a friend who cares.[7]

This world is full of people who are hurting and desperately need to experience the love and peace of God. We are called to be His hands and feet, sharing His compassion and pointing others to the unshakable foundation of His love. No matter what challenges come our way, we can stand firm, knowing that His covenant of peace is secure.

Reflect and Pray

1. Where have you recently witnessed a lack of compassion? When was the last time you could have shown mercy or compassion, but didn't?

2. How do you typically respond when someone shows you no compassion? Do you ever consider that they might be going through a hurtful experience that affects their mood?

3. The biblical book of Lamentations is a series of laments that graphically describe a terrible time in Judah's history—when the Babylonians conquered Jerusalem, burned the temple, and carried many of the people away into exile. Yet the much-quoted passage that opens this devotional stands out right in the heart of this sorrowful book. Can you think of a time when you were facing horrible circumstances, yet saw clearly the love and mercy of God that carried you through them?

4. In what ways have you been God's hands and feet lately? How do you feel when you're willingly serving others out of a love of God?

5. According to Lamentations, God's mercies are "new every morning." Try taking time the first thing every morning this week to acknowledge God's love and compassion from the day before. At the end of a week, see if the recognition of His mercies is making a difference in your faith . . . and your attitude.

When Mercy Becomes Tangible

> "Is not this the fast that I choose: to loose the bonds of wickedness, to undo the straps of the yoke, to let the oppressed go free, and to break every yoke? Is it not to share your bread with the hungry and bring the homeless poor into your house; when you see the naked, to cover him, and not to hide yourself from your own flesh?"
>
> ISAIAH 58:6-7

As we wrap up this week that has focused on mercy, I want to affirm that God's mercy is truly boundless. He offers us forgiveness and understanding that go far beyond anything we can imagine. He invites us to return to Him, no matter how far away we've wandered, and He promises to freely pardon us.

But I have to be honest: walking in the knowledge of His goodness and mercy isn't always easy. I've experienced moments where I know in my head that God is merciful, but my heart struggles to fully rest in that truth. Life has a way of clouding our perspective. When we're facing overwhelming demands of daily life, personal failures, or the brokenness we encounter in the world around us, it can sometimes feel hard to hold onto the truth of His boundless mercy.

I've seen this in others, too—a disconnect between believing in God's goodness and actually feeling it in the midst of life's challenges. Yet, even in those moments, God's mercy remains steady, waiting to break through our doubts and show us His unfailing love once again.

One of the best ways I've found to stay connected with God's goodness is to keep trying to pass it on to others. When Jesus speaks about caring for "the least of these" (Matthew 25:35-40), the Greek word He uses for "caring" describes acts of mercy and compassion, like giving to the poor or helping those in need. What's so beautiful about this word is that it's not just about feeling sympathy; it's about taking action.

Mercy becomes tangible when we clothe the naked, feed the hungry, and welcome the stranger. Jesus shows us that these acts of love are not just good deeds—they are deeply spiritual and personal to Him. He says, "Whatever you did for one of the least of these brothers and sisters of mine, you did for me." Showing mercy is a reflection of God's heart, and it's how we participate in His work of redemption. It challenges us to move beyond good intentions and step into purposeful action, meeting the needs of others with the same compassion we've received from God.

The better we come to understand God's goodness and mercy, the clearer our perspective comes during times of difficulty and opportunity. C.S. Lewis noted that "To be a Christian means to forgive the inexcusable, because God has forgiven the inexcusable in you."[8] When we reflect on how merciful He is with us, it becomes easier to extend that mercy to others. Instead of reacting to the anger around us, we can choose to be patient, kind, and understanding, even when it's not easy. That's how we reflect His love in a world that desperately needs it.

The mercy God offers is truly extraordinary. It's not something we can earn; it's a gift freely given. In a world where so many things feel conditional—where we often have to prove ourselves or make amends—God's goodness and forgiveness is refreshingly different. His mercy wipes away our mistakes and gives us a clean slate, allowing us to walk forward without the weight of guilt or shame. This kind of mercy changes us, softens our hearts, and makes it easier to extend forgiveness to others.

As we end our second week of studying God's goodness and mercy, let's pause and think about how our greater understanding of and reflection on these attributes can impact our daily living. Consider both those closest to you and those whom you regularly encounter but who may not make life easy for you. God invites us to love all people, showing compassion to those who need it most.

Reflect and Pray

1. Reread Isaiah 58:6-7. How does this passage challenge you to think about how you love and serve others?

2. How can your acts of kindness and generosity become part of your worship?

3. How does Jesus' teaching about caring for "the least of these" affect your understanding of God's goodness and mercy?

4. What specific steps can you take this week to show God's mercy and compassion to someone in need?

5. Take a few moments to focus your thoughts exclusively on the mercy of God, and how it relates to His goodness, compassion, and forgiveness. Consider how your life might be different if God wasn't merciful, and then praise Him because He is.

WEEK 3

Jesus, the Ultimate Expression of God's Goodness

Megan Allison

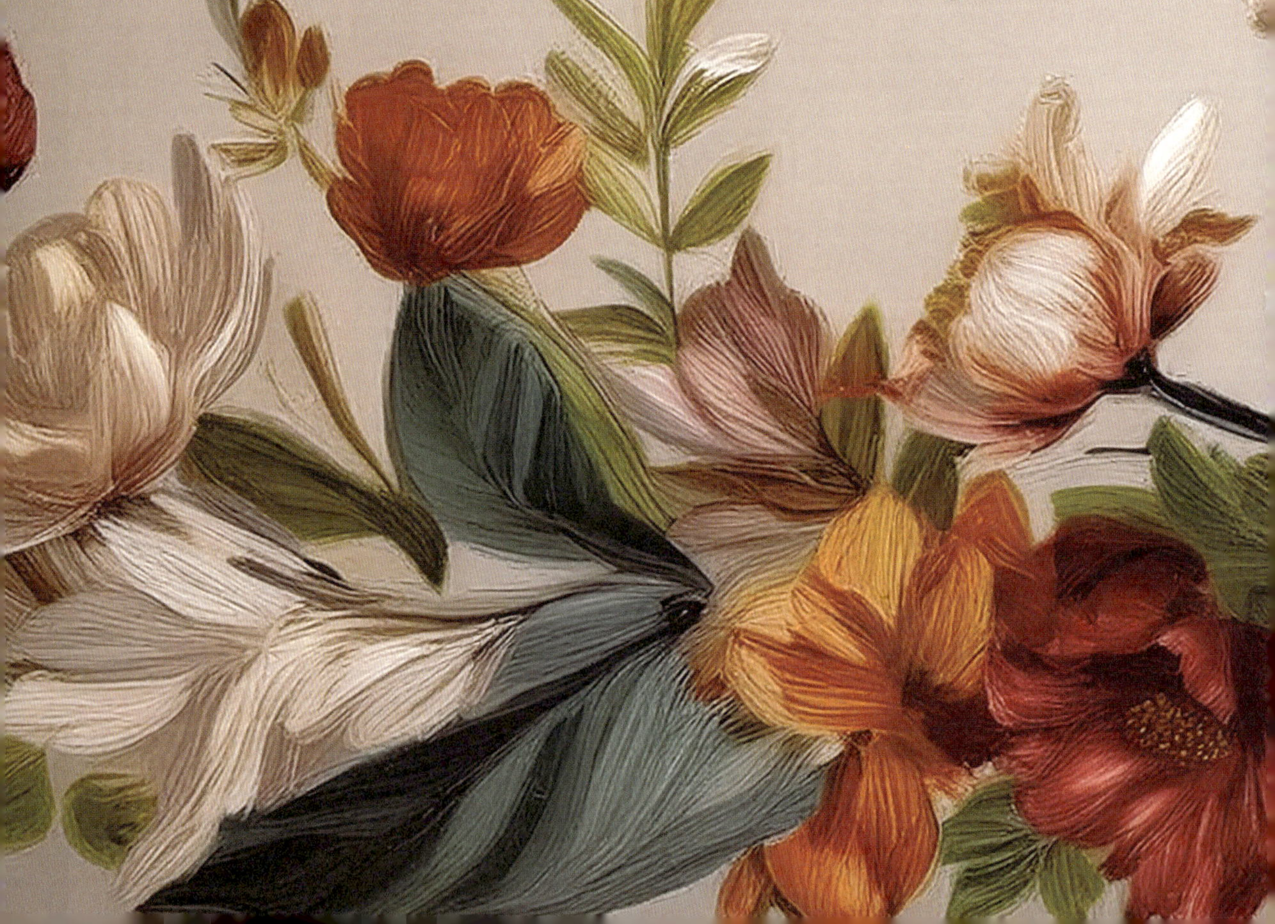

It has been such a joy to write these reflections with my mom (Julie). Working on this book together has allowed us to talk deeply about God's goodness and mercy in ways that I will always cherish. As a mother of two girls, I love seeing how my mom is not only my mentor in faith but also an amazing grandmother (Gigi) to my daughters. The way she invests her time, love, and energy into our family is such a powerful reminder of God's goodness. To have her by my side as we reflect on God's mercy—both through Jesus' example and in our own lives—is a gift. I hope that you find these reflections as meaningful as we did while writing them.

This week we are focusing on Jesus, the ultimate expression of God's goodness. We'll see how He embodies mercy, not just as an attitude of the heart, but in action. Each day we will explore how Jesus' mercy meets us in our brokenness, transforms us into people who extend grace to others, and serves as a light that shines into every dark place. Whether it's binding up the brokenhearted, inviting us to live merciful lives, or reminding us that He is the eternal Word made flesh, Jesus exemplifies the fullness of God's love for humanity.

I've found it fascinating—and quite powerful—to see how mercy was viewed by different cultures during biblical times. Roman values emphasized qualities like courage, loyalty, and reputation, with a heavy focus on honor and duty to family and state. They didn't consider mercy as a positive trait; it was often considered a weakness, or perhaps a leader might grant mercy strategically to demonstrate his power. It's a sharp contrast to what we find in the Jewish and Christian traditions, where mercy takes center stage.

Jewish values, guided by the Torah, placed a strong emphasis on justice, mercy, and humility. For example, Micah asks (and then immediately answers) a probing question: "What does the Lord require of you? To act justly and to love mercy and to walk humbly with your God" (Micah 6:8, NIV). He explains that mercy is more than a nice idea; it was central to a covenant relationship with God and was expected to shape how people treated each other, especially the vulnerable. This concept of mercy wasn't about showing power but about embodying God's compassion. It's a different kind of strength.

Then, along came Jesus who took this emphasis on mercy even further, making it one of the core virtues of the Christian faith. He taught us that mercy goes beyond obligation—it's about transforming our hearts to reflect God's love and grace, even toward those who might oppose us. The parables of the Good Samaritan and the Prodigal Son remind us that mercy triumphs over strict justice and calls us to be compassionate in ways that may seem radical, even counter-cultural. For followers of Jesus, mercy isn't just an action; it's an essential part of who we are called to be. It's so humbling to think that, in God's eyes, true strength and dignity lie in our capacity for compassion and mercy. We'll focus this week on how to deepen our understanding of what it means to live out the goodness and mercy of God through Christ.

Mercy for the Brokenhearted

"Come to me, all who labor and are heavy laden, and I will give you rest. Take my yoke upon you, and learn from me, for I am gentle and lowly in heart, and you will find rest for your souls. For my yoke is easy, and my burden is light."

MATTHEW 11:28-30

I WORK IN DERMATOLOGY where I regularly meet clients who want to restore beauty by eliminating the skin conditions that plague them—acne, eczema, rosacea, and more. Many of the skin issues are, at best, uncomfortable and, at worst, painful or dangerous if left untreated! I want to help my clients address their immediate concerns, but I also try to provide information on how they can feel even better than they did before. It is so rewarding when a client needs relief from a problem and I am able to not only provide treatment but also suggest a new sunscreen or provide information about hydration's impact on skin health. I love it when clients leave my office having traded their concerns and problems for health and beauty.

What I get to do in my practice is a very small picture of what Jesus does for us. His promise that opened today's devotion is an invitation to give Him our burdens, take on His yoke, and receive rest for your soul. For all you non-farmers, a yoke is a device that binds two animals (usually oxen) together to pull a heavy load. When we stop trying to carry all our burdens on our own and trust Jesus to bear them with us, our load is immediately lighter.

A similar promise was made in the 61st chapter of Isaiah, a prophecy about Jesus coming as Messiah:

> "The Spirit of the Sovereign Lord is on me, because the Lord has anointed me to proclaim good news to the poor. He has sent me

to bind up the brokenhearted, to proclaim freedom for the captives and release from darkness for the prisoners, to proclaim the year of the Lord's favor and the day of vengeance of our God, to comfort all who mourn, and provide for those who grieve in Zion—to bestow on them a crown of beauty instead of ashes, the oil of joy instead of mourning, and a garment of praise instead of a spirit of despair." (Isaiah 61:1-3, NIV)

This passage is a promise of coming hope, healing, restoration, freedom, and comfort, and Jesus later applies this description to himself (Luke 4:16-21). These are promises we can claim for strength today. I love to consider that Jesus:

» Binds up the brokenhearted;

» Proclaims freedom for captives and prisoners;

» Comforts those who mourn;

» Trades beauty for ashes;

» And more! What other promises do you see in these verses?

When we cry out in pain to Him, Jesus not only comforts us, He also provides us hope. He not only restores, He also renews. We are not only released from the hold of the darkness, we also find more beauty and joy in His light than we could even imagine without Him. He trades His beauty for our ashes.

Ladies, let these promises sink deeply into your heart. Let these truths solidify in you today. In time, you will see that your brokenness can bring you closer to Jesus than you might ever achieve otherwise. That was the experience of psychiatrist Gerald May. He wrote,

Blessings sometimes come through brokenness that could never come in any other way. In reflecting on my own life, I have to conclude that grace has come through me more powerfully sometimes when I have been very dysfunctional and maladjusted. Love transcends all possible adjustments and continually invites us through and beyond them.[9]

Whatever burden you may carry—a broken relationship, a dream that hasn't yet come to fruition, the weariness of simply holding it all together, or whatever it might be—know this: Jesus sees you. He meets you in those places that feel too heavy to bear. His mercy is not just a theological concept; it is a personal gift. He is binding your wounds, replacing your sorrow with joy, and whispering hope into the darkest corners of your soul. You are not forgotten, and your ashes will not define you. Jesus himself is exchanging them for a radiant crown of beauty.

Reflect and Pray

1. In what area(s) of your life are you currently most in need of Jesus' healing and comfort?

2. Read Isaiah 61:1-3 again. Which of those promises resonates most with you?

3. Reflect again on Matthew 11:28-30. How does Jesus' invitation to the weary relate to His role in binding up the brokenhearted?

4. How can you use the comfort God has given you to comfort others?

5. Meditate on Isaiah 61:1-3 and let its message resonate in your heart. Read the passage silently several times, and then read it aloud, slowly. Write it down and post it where you will see it frequently this week.

Blessed Are the Merciful

"Blessed are the merciful, for they shall receive mercy."

MATTHEW 5:7

ONE OF THE MOST BEAUTIFUL ASPECTS of Jesus' teachings is His invitation to embody mercy in our lives. Mercy is not just an abstract concept for us to learn about; it's deeply practical, something we live out every day. In the Beatitudes, the introduction to His Sermon on the Mount, Jesus tells us that mercy is a blessing—not only for those who receive it, but also for those who extend it. This is such an important reminder for women following Jesus.

We learn mercy by experiencing mercy and then by practicing it. Pastor Rick Warren has said, "God's mercy to us is the motivation for showing mercy to others. Remember, you will never be asked to forgive someone else more than God has forgiven you."[10] And then, as we begin to offer mercy to others, we open ourselves to experiencing God's mercy even more fully in our own lives.

The Greek word for "merciful" in Matthew 5:7 doesn't just mean feeling pity. Rather, it emphasizes mercy as an action. It conveys a deep sense of active compassion and kindness. To be merciful is to take steps to relieve the suffering or need of someone else. The same word is used in Hebrews 2:17: "Therefore [Jesus] had to be made like his brothers in every respect, so that he might become a merciful and faithful high priest in the service of God, to make propitiation [atonement] for the sins of the people."

Mercy is not passive but is deeply tied to reflecting God's heart through action. Jesus highlighted this in His teachings and modeled it throughout His compassionate life, showing that extending mercy allows us to participate in the divine nature of God's love.

As a dermatology provider, I try to extend mercy when patients come to me feeling self-conscious or frustrated with their skin conditions. It's a privilege to listen, offer support, and provide solutions that can help them feel more confident. As a mom, I'm constantly finding opportunities to practice mercy. Whether it's showing patience with my kids when they've spilled something for the third time that day or grabbing an extra diaper from my bag for a mom who forgot to bring one to the park, I'm reminded that mercy is about more than just kindness. Mercy often requires us to put aside our pride, step into someone else's shoes, and act with compassion, even when it's hard. For busy and exhausted moms, the challenge in showing mercy means slowing down and looking beyond the demands placed on us from moment to moment.

I often pray for God to help me see the world with His merciful eyes, and He frequently shows me that mercy is not always about grand gestures. Often, it's shown through small, intentional acts of kindness that let someone know they are valued and seen. I cited Micah 6:8 in this week's introduction, but it's especially relevant here: "And what does the Lord require of you? To act justly and to love mercy and to walk humbly with your God."

You might be surprised at what happens if you begin to consistently show mercy to others in small ways. The author of Hebrews challenges us: "Do not forget to show hospitality to strangers, for by so doing some people have shown hospitality to angels without knowing it" (Hebrews 13:1-2). What an incredible thought! Mercy opens the door for unexpected blessings, not just for others, but for us as well. We may never know the full impact of a merciful act, but God does.

Remember that when you choose mercy, you reflect the goodness of God, and in doing so, you draw closer to Him.

Reflect and Pray

1. Who are some people you know who need God's mercy, and how might you be able to help them experience it?

2. How can showing kindness and compassion draw *you* closer to God?

3. How does God's challenge in Micah 6:8 emphasize mercy as a priority in the calling of His people?

4. If you're being honest, are there times when showing kindness and compassion feels challenging, or even difficult? Explain.

5. Take a moment to reflect on how showing mercy might become more frequent in your daily life. Who in your life needs to experience God's mercy through you?

The Word Became Flesh

**The Word became flesh and dwelt among us,
and we have seen his glory, glory as of the only Son from the
Father, full of grace and truth.**

JOHN 1:14

I'M OFTEN STRUCK BY HOW PERSONAL and tangible God's love is, especially within family life. It's one thing to hear "I love you," but it's something else entirely when love is expressed through actions—whether it's a hug, a helping hand, or a thoughtful gesture. Love in action is what makes John 1:14 such a powerful verse to me. God's love wasn't just spoken; it wasn't just described in the written record; it was made real when Jesus, the Word, became flesh and lived among us.

When I think about this verse, I try to imagine what seeing Him in person must have been like. Those who saw Him face-to-face got to see His glory—the glory of the one and only Son. Through Him, they experienced God's grace and truth firsthand. What a gift to know that God didn't stay distanced or detached, but chose to enter our world, walk with us, and show us what God's goodness looks like in action.

Jesus' choice to take on human form is even more remarkable when we consider His humility in doing so. When urging his readers to be more humble, the Apostle Paul used Jesus as the ultimate example to follow:

> Do nothing from selfish ambition or conceit, but in humility count others more significant than yourselves. Let each of you look not only to his own interests, but also to the interests of others. Have this mind among yourselves, which is yours in Christ Jesus, who, though he was in the form of God, did not count equality with God

a thing to be grasped, but emptied himself, by taking the form of a servant, being born in the likeness of men. And being found in human form, he humbled himself by becoming obedient to the point of death, even death on a cross. (Philippians 2:3-8)

Jesus was fully God, yet He didn't cling to His equality with God. Instead, He became a servant and lived among us as a human being. He humbled himself to the point of dying on a cross for our sake. That degree of love and humility is overwhelming to consider. Jesus could have come as a king with armies or riches, yet He came as one of us, offering grace and truth through His presence. His willingness to set aside His glory for our salvation demonstrates just how deeply He loves us.

I find tremendous comfort in knowing that Jesus understands what it's like to live in this world. Augustine expressed this truth in a most emphatic way:

Man's maker was made man that He, Ruler of the stars, might nurse at His mother's breast; that the Bread might hunger, the Fountain thirst, the Light sleep, the Way be tired on His journey; that the Truth might be accused of false witness, the Teacher be beaten with whips, the Foundation be suspended on wood; that Strength might grow weak; that the Healer might be wounded; that Life might die.[11]

When I feel overwhelmed, I remember that Jesus knows what it's like to feel joy, pain, exhaustion, and every other human emotion. He is right there with me. His presence isn't just something to read about—it's a reality to experience.

What's the best way to experience God's presence? No doubt at some point in your life you've seen bracelets, bumper stickers, or other merchandise emblazoned with WWJD. For more than a century now, believers have been challenged to ask "What would Jesus do?" when faced with problems, difficult choices, or moral dilemmas. The question forces us to take what we know about the biblical Jesus we read about, and then mentally place Him in a modern-day situation. Perhaps this approach might be helpful at times to help you envision God's presence in your life.

And for me, studying God's Word has consistently been a reliable starting point for sensing the nearness of Jesus. Through Scripture, we not only learn about Jesus' life, but we also see His character, hear His promises, and witness His love for us revealed.

Just as Jesus is described as the Word made flesh, the Bible provides a tangible way to connect with Him today. When we take the time to engage with God's written Word—whether through reading, meditation, or study—we invite His living Word to dwell in our hearts and transform our lives. A growing knowledge and love of Scripture equips us with the wisdom and strength we need to navigate life's challenges with grace and faith.

Reflect and Pray

1. In your own words, how would you explain the phrase, "The Word became flesh"?

2. How does realizing that Jesus once lived among us affect the way you perceive God's love for you?

3. Review Philippians 2:3-8. How does Jesus' humility in setting aside His divine privileges challenge the mindset you have about serving others?

4. Can you think of specific areas of your life that would benefit from an increased level of humility and selflessness?

5. This week, take some time to reflect on what it means that Jesus became flesh and made His dwelling among us. How does knowing He is with you change the way you approach your challenges? How can you invite Him to dwell more fully in your heart and your daily life?

In the Beginning with the Word

In the beginning was the Word, and the Word was with God, and the Word was God. He was in the beginning with God. All things were made through him, and without him was not any thing made that was made.

JOHN 1:1-3

ON DAY 1 OF WEEK 1 OF THIS SERIES, Mom noted that God has always existed. I must agree with her that it's definitely a hard concept for me to wrap my mind around. And another awe-inspiring truth is that Jesus was always right there with Him. This fact is confirmed by today's passage from John. Since Jesus was with God in the beginning and was involved in Creation, He must have been here *before* the "beginning." Jesus' human life may have begun in the manger in Bethlehem, but He has *always* existed.

The Greek word *logos*, translated as "Word" in John 1:1, carries profound meaning that bridges cultural and theological contexts. In Greek philosophy, *logos* referred to reason, wisdom, or the principle that brought order and meaning to the universe. To Jewish readers, *logos* is connected to the powerful Word of God in creation and revelation, as described in Genesis 1 and Psalm 33:6-7: "By the word of the Lord the heavens were made, and by the breath of his mouth all their host. He gathers the waters of the sea as a heap; he puts the deeps in storehouses."

John takes this concept even further, declaring that Jesus is not just a messenger or a part of creation but the *logos* himself—the divine reason and creative power made flesh. This means that Jesus embodies God's wisdom, speaks with His authority, and sustains all things. The Word that spoke the world into being once walked the earth with us and continues to live in our hearts, showing us the fullness of God's goodness and love.

As a dermatology provider, I often find myself marveling at the intricacies of creation—from the way our bodies are designed to the beauty of a sunrise. I am filled with gratitude to realize that Jesus was part of creating it all. He didn't just create the world; He created us, and He knows every detail of each individual's life.

This passage also reminds me of the firm foundation we have in Jesus. Because He was there in the beginning, we can trust Him to be with us in every moment. He holds our lives together with His steadfast love, guiding us through the uncertainties and challenges we face.

This truth is echoed in Revelation 1:8, where the Lord declares, "I am the Alpha and the Omega, who is and who was and who is to come, the Almighty." Jesus, as the Alpha, was present at creation, and as the Omega, He will bring all things to fulfillment. He was the foundation of all things, and He is the One who holds the future in His hands. The author of Hebrews offers us the assurance that "Jesus Christ is the same yesterday and today and forever" (Hebrews 13:8). His eternal nature gives us the confidence to trust Him completely, knowing He is unchanging and always faithful, from the beginning of time to the end.

Reflect and Pray

1. Knowing that Jesus is the eternal Word of God and has been active from the beginning (since before Creation), what foundations can you establish in your life and faith?

2. How does knowing that Jesus is both the Alpha and the Omega—the beginning and the end—help you find peace in the uncertainties of your life?

3. Does it affect your faith and trust in Jesus in any way to realize that He is the same yesterday, today, and forever? If so, how?

4. Review Psalm 33:6-7. What attributes of God stand out to you in this passage?

5. Take some time today to reflect on the incredible truths that Jesus, the Word, was here from the beginning and that He never changes. Whether this is new information to you or simply a reminder, how will you respond?

Unquenchable Light

**The light shines in the darkness,
and the darkness has not overcome it.**

JOHN 1:5

As a mom, I'm often reminded how much children dislike the dark—or, really, how much they don't want to be alone in the dark. At bedtime, my girls always ask for a nightlight, and when we travel, I make sure we pack one. That little bit of light makes a big difference for them, and honestly, even as an adult I'll admit to feeling a lot more comfortable if I have a light when everything else is pitch black.

This truth about physical light mirrors a greater spiritual truth: Jesus is the light that shines in the darkness. The context of John 1:5 is deeply tied to the grand introduction of Jesus as the Word of God. In the opening verses of John's Gospel, we see a beautiful and poetic declaration of who Jesus is. John begins by taking us back to the very beginning, reminding us that Jesus, the Word, was with God and was God. He establishes that through Jesus, all things were made, and nothing exists apart from Him.

Then, John introduces an essential truth: Jesus is life, and that life is the light of all humankind. This light is not just any light—it is divine, eternal, and unquenchable. John 1:5 reminds us that we place our hope in a light that shines in the darkness, and the darkness cannot overcome it. Darkness, representing sin, chaos, and separation from God, does not stand a chance against the light of Christ.

No matter how dark your life gets, be it from the influence of evil people, emotional distress, physical decline, or whatever, Jesus' light can never be extinguished. Jesus' goodness and presence bring hope to the darkest moments of our lives, providing peace and reassurance that no degree of darkness can snuff out.

One of my favorite times to read my Bible is early in the morning before anyone else in the house is awake. My purple Bible and my cup of coffee are part of a routine that centers me for the day ahead. Winter mornings provide a special stillness that feels both peaceful and holy. I get up when it's still dark, yet I know that very soon nothing will stop the light of morning from driving the darkness away. Over the years, I've grown to cherish this quiet time because I know I'm not alone—I'm sitting in the light of God's presence.

That light of Christ isn't just figurative. It's real and tangible. Jesus' presence brings clarity, warmth, and peace to those dark places in our lives that can feel overwhelming. Whether it's the darkness of uncertainty, fear, grief, or pain, His light shines, reminding us that we are never alone.

M. Scott Peck famously wrote, "Life is difficult." Yet Jesus doesn't leave us in despair. He reassures us that He has already overcome the troubles of this world. His victory over darkness gives us the confidence to face challenges, knowing that His light is greater than any difficulty we might encounter.

Later in his Gospel, John reminds us of something else Jesus promised: "I have said these things to you, that in me you may have peace. In the world you will have tribulation. But take heart; I have overcome the world" (John 16:33). Then, in John's first letter, he addresses how these truths should influence our relationships with God and other people: "God is light, and in him is no darkness at all. If we say we have fellowship with him while we walk in darkness, we lie and do not practice the truth. But if we walk in the light, as he is in the light, we have fellowship with one another, and the blood of Jesus his Son cleanses us from all sin" (1 John 1:5-7).

In closing, let's be clear about one thing: our verse for today doesn't say that light competes with darkness. It's no contest! Scripture boldly declares that darkness cannot overcome the light of Christ. This sets the stage for the rest of John's Gospel, which reveals Jesus as the Light of the World, bringing life, truth, and salvation to all who believe. In a world that often feels heavy with darkness, this verse is a powerful reminder that Jesus' light is stronger, brighter, and eternal. The hope it provides isn't just for someday—it's for today, offering peace and clarity no matter how overwhelming life may feel.

Jesus is the light. Darkness cannot overcome Him. What an incredible reassurance!

Reflect and Pray

1. In what areas of your life do you see the need to more fully embrace Jesus' light, leaving behind any areas where fear, doubt, or sin might linger?

2. How would greater confidence that the light of Jesus overcomes *all* darkness affect your level of hope?

3. Does it bother you that Jesus assures us that in the world we *will* face tribulation (John 16:33)? Why or why not?

4. Review 1 John 1:5-7. How does walking in the light bring fellowship with God and others?

5. Think back over the content you've covered this week. How have these sessions helped you better understand how Jesus is the ultimate expression of God's goodness? Ask God to heighten and deepen your experience of His goodness.

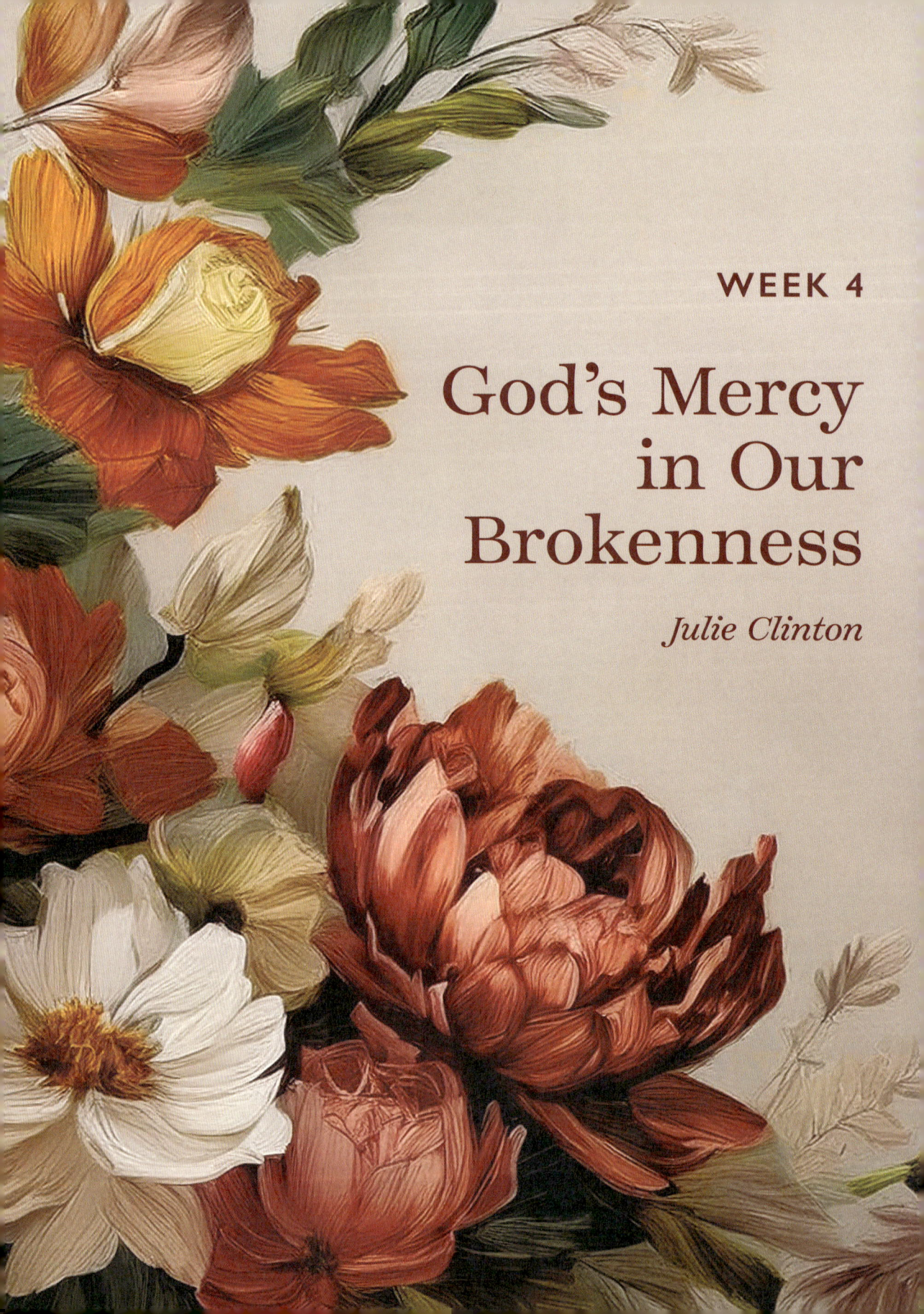

WEEK 4

God's Mercy in Our Brokenness

Julie Clinton

IN TODAY'S WORLD, WE OFTEN FEEL PULLED between faith and fear. As I reflect on this tension, I'm reminded of something my son, Zach, shared on his podcast, *Built Different*: The letters in the word "faith" symbolize "Fully And Intently Trusting Him," while "fear" is "False Evidence Appearing Real." Faith and fear both focus on a future that hasn't happened yet, but they lead us in opposite directions. Fear pulls us into worry and despair, while faith leads us into trust and hope.

Some people mistakenly believe that faith protects them from difficulties, but even a casual reading of the Scriptures shows that a faithful commitment to God sometimes leads us directly into struggles, and in every trial we face, faith reframes the hardship. Let me point to just two examples: Paul was zealous in his dedication to Christ and the Great Commission, but his commitment didn't shield him from trouble. In fact, he suffered beatings, stoning, imprisonment, and rejection from all sides, as well as hunger and thirst. At one point, he was so discouraged that it seemed he welcomed death. He wrote, "For we were so utterly burdened beyond our strength that we despaired of life itself. Indeed, we felt that we had received the sentence of death. But that was to make us rely not on ourselves but on God who raises the dead" (2 Corinthians 1:8-9). But Paul learned that God will use our heartaches, flaws, and limitations to deepen our faith and shape our character. To the believers in Rome, he explained that faith in Jesus gives us peace with God, but he didn't stop there: "Not only that, but we rejoice in our sufferings, knowing that suffering produces endurance, and endurance produces character, and character produces hope, and hope does not put us to shame, because God's love has been poured into our hearts through the Holy Spirit who has been given to us" (Romans 5:3-5). We can't always (or even often) see God's grand purposes for everything that happens to us, but we can trust Him even when we don't understand.

The second example is Jesus. No one has been (or could be) more dedicated to the Father, but Jesus' faith and love led Him into rejection, betrayal, suffering, and death. In Gethsemane, Jesus asked the Father to provide another way to pay for the sins of the world, but there was no other way. What kept Him strong as he faced the punishment of hell deserved by every human who has ever or will ever live? After the writer to the Hebrews gives us a litany of heroes of the faith, he points to the supreme hero: "Therefore, since we are surrounded by so great a cloud of witnesses, let us also lay aside every weight, and sin which clings so closely, and let us run with endurance the race that is set before us, looking to Jesus, the founder and perfecter of our faith, who for the joy that was set before him endured the cross, despising the shame, and is seated at the right hand of the throne of God" (Hebrews 12:1-2). He was thinking of us!

Our sense of brokenness can come from many directions: We may have been betrayed by someone we trusted, abandoned by someone we love, devastated by disease or the death of someone close to us, the fragility of chronic anxiety, or the crushing weight of depression, among countless other causes. I hope you don't feel broken today, but as I've talked to women over the years (and looked in the mirror), I've come to the conclusion that all of us experience three tenses of brokenness: We have suffered in the past, we're suffering now, or we'll surely suffer in the future.

If you're struggling, it's not because God has abandoned you or that He's punishing you. The cross shows that all the punishment we deserve has been poured out on Jesus! We're free, forgiven, and adored. You may feel distant from Him, but He's as close as your breath.

I see the dynamic of overcoming fear with my granddaughters, Olivia and Sophia. They can name their fears even in their innocence—like spiders or fictional characters. Mario and Luigi have become popular with kids again, and Olivia dresses up as a precious Princess Peach. If you ask her what she fears, she will widen her eyes and say that she's afraid of Bowser, the fictional turtle-like leader and Mario's evil nemesis. While her response is funny and adorable, Oliva's proclamation of Bowser as "so scary" reminds me that fear begins early. Thankfully, so does the opportunity to nurture faith. As long as Olivia has Gigi (or Mommy, Daddy, or Papa), she isn't that scared. Just as we provide an environment where our children feel safe and loved, God's mercy draws us close, assuring us of His presence and provision.

This week, we'll begin by exploring how God's mercy brings us both grace and truth in Christ, a truth that changes everything about how we live. Next, we'll turn to the incredible gift of His Son Jesus and God's plan for salvation, not condemnation. On Day 3, we'll dive into the powerful imagery of Jesus as "the light of the world," shining into the darkest corners of our lives. From there, we'll explore the challenging but transformative topic of forgiveness—part of God's merciful nature. Through the story of the woman caught in adultery, we'll see how Jesus' mercy offers us the freedom to lay down our stones—whether they're directed at others or ourselves. Finally, we'll close the week with a reminder of Jesus' healing power as He meets us in our brokenness and invites us into a life of hope and renewal.

We all have "Bowsers" in our lives. As we journey through this week, remember God's unshakable mercy. Whether you're navigating fear, brokenness, or uncertainty, His mercy is always greater. Let's trust Him to meet us right where we are and guide us into a deeper understanding of His love.

DAY I

Mercy and Truth in Christ

**For the law was given through Moses;
grace and truth came through Jesus Christ.**

JOHN 1:17

GRACE AND MERCY ARE SIBLINGS: mercy means "we don't get the punishment we deserve," and grace means "we get the love, honor, and acceptance we don't deserve." Thankfully, both are poured out in abundance on us!

Christmas is one of my favorite seasons, partly because it reminds me so much of God's goodness and mercy. Our family makes a special trip with Olivia and Sophia to The Greenbrier each year for their magical "Dinner in Whoville." It's one of those traditions that feels like stepping into a storybook. We take horse-drawn carriage rides through the grounds, wrapped in big, cozy blankets. When we return, there's always the sweet aroma of hot chocolate wafting through the air as Santa makes his grand entrance. Olivia calls The Greenbriar "the Christmas hotel" and is ready to return for the next year before we've even left! These moments feel sacred, filled with light and love, reminding me of how special and magical life can be, even in the middle of hard times.

We don't just establish these traditions with our kids and grandkids to create beautiful memories; we also want to show them a tangible picture of God's mercy. Christmas transforms ordinary days into something special. In the same way, God's mercy transforms our broken, ordinary lives into something extraordinary. Christmas is a reminder that God's mercy is more than just a feeling—it's active, redemptive, and deeply personal. Through the birth of Jesus, God offered us His grace and truth, inviting us into a story of hope and redemption greater than we can imagine.

While I love every part of our annual "Christmas hotel" tradition, my favorite moment is always looking up at the starry sky during the carriage ride. There's something so peaceful about seeing the night lit with countless stars. It always makes me think of the angels who appeared to the shepherds to announce the birth of Christ. The shepherds were ordinary people doing their jobs in the fields, yet they were the first to hear the incredible news of Jesus' birth. That night, heaven touched the earth, and everything changed.

The beauty of the incarnation—and the message of John 1:17—is that God didn't just give us the law through Moses and say, "Good luck with that!" The law was never meant to be the full picture. It shows us that we sin, "missing the target" of God's goodness and holiness, and revealing our need for a Savior. The sacrifices in the law pointed to the ultimate sacrifice: the sinless Son of God who paid the price we couldn't pay and lived the life we couldn't live. The law paved the way to the fulfillment of God's plan "in the fullness of time": when God became a human being and walked among us.

I see God's mercy so clearly in the Christmas story. The people of God were living under the heel of Rome—exiles in their own land. They'd suffered mistreatment for generations, and they longed for the Messiah to rescue them. They were brokenhearted. Many believed the Messiah would be a great military commander who would lead God's army against the Roman legions, but God had other plans. God could have chosen a grand palace for His Son's arrival, but instead, Jesus was born in a stable. The King of Kings was laid in a manger, wrapped in strips of cloth that were similar to the ones used three decades later to wrap His lifeless body before putting it in Joseph's tomb. What an incredible picture of tender mercy and limitless grace!

Today, we see much anger and resentment all around us. I'm afraid that many Christians are just as angry and resentful as unbelievers. We're vessels filled with something; when we're jostled, whatever fills us spills out. We need to fill our hearts with God's kindness, goodness, truth, and grace so that when anything bumps us, the character of Christ spills out.

God's people at the time of the incarnation felt broken and abandoned, but God hadn't forgotten them. Christmas is a picture of God's mercy and grace meeting us where we are, even in the messiness and simplicity of our lives. When the angels announced the birth of Jesus, they proclaimed, "Peace on earth, goodwill toward men." We need that peace and goodwill today.

But we don't have to wait for the Christmas season to reflect on God's mercy toward us and ways we can show mercy to others. The message of Christmas is for every day of our lives: Emmanuel, "God with us," has arrived in all of His beauty, power, mercy, truth, and grace—even on our darkest days.

Reflect and Pray

1. What are some ways the law of Moses pointed to the Messiah's coming?

2. Paraphrase the statement: Jesus took the punishment we deserve so we could receive the love, honor, and acceptance He deserves.

3. Read Titus 2:11-14. How does Paul describe the impact of grace in the life of believers?

4. Think of a time in the last few days when you were "bumped" by a disappointment, a delay, or some other disruption. What spilled out? If it wasn't God's love, kindness, and mercy, does your response bother you? What will you do about it?

5. Ask God to fill you with a deeper grasp of His mercy and grace.

God's Merciful Gift of His Son

**"For God so loved the world that he gave his one
and only Son, that whoever believes in him shall not perish
but have eternal life."**

JOHN 3:16

THIS IS THE BEST-KNOWN AND MOST-QUOTED VERSE in the Bible, but familiarity can numb us to its rich meaning. We can think, *Yeah, yeah, I know. God loves us. What's next?* Perhaps we need a refresher course on the truth that we don't deserve God's love. In Romans 5, Paul gives a very unflattering picture of our condition apart from God's love: people are "weak," "sinners," and "enemies" of God (Romans 5:6-10). We may not want to think about it, but we deserved God's judgment and condemnation. To the degree that we grasp our unworthiness, we'll be amazed at the love and grace of God!

A little later in Paul's letter, he asks the ultimate question: "Wretched man that I am! Who will deliver me from this body of death?" And he answers this desperate question with clarity: "Thanks be to God through Jesus Christ our Lord! . . . There is therefore now no condemnation for those who are in Christ Jesus" (Romans 7:24-8:1).

God's love for sinners (like you and me) is the most astounding truth in history! Three and a half centuries ago, the Puritan Thomas Manton preached a sermon on John 3:16. He invited his listeners to be amazed that God could and would love us so dearly. Let me quote him at length:

> Love is at the bottom of all. We may give a reason of other things,
> but we cannot give a reason of his love. God showed his wisdom,
> power, justice, and holiness in our redemption by Christ. If you ask,
> Why he made so much ado about a worthless creature, raised out
> of the dust of the ground at first, and had now disordered himself,

76 | NEW EVERY MORNING

and could be of no use to him? We have an answer at hand, Because he loved us. If you continue to ask, But why did he love us? We have no other answer but because he loved us; for beyond the first rise of things we cannot go. And the same reason is given by Moses, Deuteronomy 7:7-8: "The Lord did not set his love upon you, nor choose you, because you were more in number than any people, for ye were the fewest of all people; but because the Lord loved you …" That is, in short, he loved you because he loved you. All came from his free and undeserved mercy; higher we cannot go in seeking after the causes of what is done for our salvation.[12]

How can we grasp a love so high and wide and deep? God has given us two sources of understanding: the family and the Holy Spirit. God's design for the family is a hot-house of love so that as children grow up, they can say, "The love of God must be like, and even greater, than the love my mother and father have shown me." Those who feel their parents' strong affection can more easily trust that God adores them too. But all of us—those from loving families and the rest of us—need the Spirit of God to awaken our hearts to experience God's matchless love. The Spirit then uses our new family of brothers and sisters to demonstrate God's affection for us.

Yesterday's devotional reminded me of the joy and connection I feel during our family's Christmas celebrations. So, whatever time of year you read my words, let's take our thoughts again to the Christmas season. Tim comes from a large pastor's family—eight kids in all—and we host the Clinton clan every year the weekend before Christmas. With 50 to 60 family members filling our home, it's a whirlwind of laughter, love, and cherished traditions. We sing carols, hand out door prizes, and honor Tim's dad's legacy by reading the Christmas story together. Come to think of it, the door prizes started with Tim's dad, too. They're simple gifts—aprons, flashlights—but they bring such joy to the evening.

Not everyone has that kind of family experience. For some, brokenness comes from separation, conflict, or the deep ache of loss. Maybe you've never had those kinds of supportive connections in your family. My heart goes out to you, and I hope you feel how loved and prayed for you are as part of the Extraordinary Women family. More importantly, you are part of God's family, brought into eternal community through Jesus' sacrifice. You are welcomed in, no longer an outsider.

Many times when we read or hear John 3:16, we stop without reading the next verse: "For God did not send his Son into the world to condemn the world, but to save the world through him" (John 3:17). Verse 16 shows the *depth* of God's love, and verse 17 reveals the *purpose* of His love—not condemnation, but salvation.

Many people, including many Christians, are haunted by past failures or deep wounds. They "beat themselves up" for being "so stupid" or "flawed" or "ugly." Accusing, condemning thoughts are their frequent companions, but John 3:17 reminds us that God's heart is not one of judgment but one of rescue. Jesus didn't come to point out all the ways we've fallen short; He came to bring us back into a relationship with Him—a relationship of deepest affection, complete safety, and wondrous delight. Mercy meets us where we are, offering redemption instead of rejection. This isn't to say that we don't need to address our sins, but God's love and mercy have washed our sins away.

Our sins have been completely forgiven. On the cross, Jesus' last words were, "It is finished," or "It is paid in full." Self-condemnation and shame don't make us more forgiven and loved! But emotional wounds take time to heal. Yes, God's love heals, but it's a process. The truth is that healing doesn't always come in the way or time we expect. Sometimes, it looks like restored relationships; other times, it's the peace to move forward even when circumstances don't change. But Jesus' love is always enough. He sees us in our pain, meets us in our need, and offers a hope that transforms.

Reflect and Pray

1. What are some signs someone has become numb to the wonder of God's love?

2. Look again at Romans 7:24-8:1. Describe Paul's desperation and relief.

3. Describe the role of the family (whether family of origin or God's forever family) in convincing us of God's love.

4. Read Romans 8:15-17. What is the Holy Spirit's role in preparing our hearts to experience the love of God?

5. Ask God to make His love more real to you than ever.

DAY 3

Jesus, the Light of the World

**When Jesus spoke again to the people, he said,
"I am the light of the world. Whoever follows me will never
walk in darkness, but will have the light of life."**

JOHN 8:12

In his Gospel, John records Jesus making seven "I am" statements. The number seven appears more than 700 times in the Bible. It represents completeness and holiness. When I think about the seven "I am" statements of Jesus, I marvel at the depth and richness of each one. They're not just poetic metaphors or theological ideas—they're vivid pictures of how Jesus meets us right where we are, offering us His mercy, provision, and presence in every moment. Each statement speaks to a specific need and reveals a unique aspect of Jesus. Let's look more closely at them:

» **"I am the bread of life" (John 6:35).**

Jesus had just fed 5,000 people (probably 15,000 to 20,000, counting women and children), and the crowd followed Him asking for more. Instead, He used bread as a metaphor for what our souls need for sustenance . . . and He is the bread that gives life.

» **"I am the light of the world" (John 8:12).**

Light shows us dangers and illuminates the path. Without it, we stumble and fall. Jesus is the source of wisdom and truth, even when the path seems uncertain.

» **"I am the door" (John 10:9).**

We might try to find meaning by walking through the doors of wealth, intelligence, comfort, power, or popularity, but Jesus is the open door to a rich, deep purpose in life.

» **"I am the good shepherd" (John 10:11).**

In Israel, religious leaders weren't fulfilling their God-given role as sources of protection and nourishment for His people. They were self-absorbed; Jesus "lays down his life for the sheep." As a mom and now a grandmother, I know what it feels like to watch over and protect the little ones I love. Jesus takes that to an entirely different level. He doesn't just guide us; He lays down His life for us—the ultimate act of mercy and love.

» **"I am the resurrection and the life" (John 11:25).**

Mary and Martha were distraught when their brother Lazarus died. Jesus told Martha not only that He could raise her brother from the grave but that He embodies that divine power. He wasn't just talking about His own victory over death—He was inviting us into a life filled with hope and renewal. I've seen this truth firsthand in seasons of loss and heartache. His resurrection power brings life to places we thought were beyond saving, reminding us that nothing is too broken for Him to restore.

» **"I am the way, the truth, and the life" (John 14:6).**

After the Last Supper, Jesus took His disciples for a walk so He could prepare them for His betrayal, arrest, trial, and crucifixion. They were understandably confused, and Thomas voiced what must have been on all their hearts: "I don't get it!" Jesus didn't give them a roadmap and a compass; He promised to be their roadmap, compass, and constant guide. In a world that pulls us in so many directions, it's tempting to search for answers in all the wrong places. But Jesus is clear—He is the way. When we trust Him, we find the truth that sets us free and the life that truly satisfies us.

» **"I am the true vine" (John 15:1).**

In Isaiah, God is depicted as the master of a vineyard, but all He got was wild grapes. Jesus is the new Israel, the true vine that produces a good harvest in those who follow Him. Jesus invites us to stay connected to Him, drawing strength and sustenance from His presence. Like a branch can't bear fruit apart from the vine, we can't thrive without abiding in Him. This has been a constant reminder for me in busy seasons—

whether it's planning a conference, preparing a devotional, or just keeping up with the demands of daily life. When I feel stretched thin, I hear His gentle whisper: "Stay connected to Me. Let My strength be your source."

These statements are more than declarations—they're invitations. Jesus invites us to experience His presence and mercy in every facet of our lives. He is the bread that feeds us, the light that guides us, the door that welcomes us, the shepherd who protects us, the resurrection that gives us hope, the way that leads us home, and the vine that sustains us.

As you reflect on these truths today, consider how Jesus is revealing himself to you right now. Is He offering nourishment for a weary heart? Light in a dark season? Guidance in a confusing time? Wherever you are, His mercy is enough.

Reflect and Pray

1. Which of Jesus' "I am" statements resonates with you today? Explain your answer.

2. How do you think the people who heard Him responded when He spoke those words? What do we know that they didn't?

3. Read John 15:1-5. What difference does it (or would it) make for you to "abide" in Christ?

4. What are some distractions that can keep you from abiding, which one person called "practicing the presence of God"?

5. Think of people you know who are struggling. Review each of these statements as you pray for them.

Mercy and Forgiveness

**"Neither do I condemn you.
Go now and leave your life of sin."**

JOHN 8:11

ONE OF THE MOST BEAUTIFUL EXAMPLES of God's mercy is found in John 8. A woman caught in adultery was brought before Jesus by those who wanted to condemn her. Yet, instead of condemnation, Jesus offered her forgiveness and freedom. He didn't excuse her sin but showed her a better way, saying, "Go now and leave your life of sin," which some translations phrase as "Go and sin no more."

When I read this passage, I often think about how we all grab stones to throw—at others and just as often, at ourselves. We live in a culture that's quick to judge and slow to forgive. Whether it's an unkind comment online, a misunderstanding with a friend, being taken for granted by a family member, or even the harsh expectations we place on ourselves, it's easy to pick up stones . . . and grabbing stones can easily become a habit when we feel threatened. But Jesus shows us a different way, one that calls us to lay down our stones and extend the same mercy we've received.

When someone hurts us, our immediate response is to create a caricature of the person in our minds. If he lied, "He's just a liar." If she was unkind, "She's always cruel." God wants us to see every person as created in His image, of inestimable value. Professor and theologian Miroslav Volf observed,

> Forgiveness flounders because I exclude the enemy from the community of humans even as I exclude myself from the community of sinners. But no one can be in the presence of the God of the crucified Messiah for long without overcoming this double exclusion—with-

out transposing the enemy from the sphere of the monstrous . . . into the sphere of shared humanity and herself from the sphere of proud innocence into the sphere of common sinfulness. When one knows [as the cross demonstrates] that the torturer will not eternally triumph over the victim, one is free to rediscover that person's humanity and imitate God's love for him. And when one knows [as the cross demonstrates] that God's love is greater than all sin, one is free to see oneself in the light of God's justice and so rediscover one's own sinfulness.[13]

Forgiveness isn't excusing ("He couldn't help it"), minimizing ("Oh, it wasn't that bad"), or denying ("I don't know what you're talking about"). Author and pastor Lewis Smedes wrote, "When we forgive evil we do not excuse it, we do not tolerate it, we do not smother it. We look the evil full in the face, call it what it is, let its horror shock and stun and enrage us, and only then do we forgive it."[14]

Forgiveness is one of the most challenging ways we live out God's mercy, but it's also one of the most powerful. I've seen this truth play out in my own life. When I feel wronged or struggle with resentment, I'm reminded of how much I've been forgiven. It's humbling to realize that if God, in His infinite goodness, can forgive me, how can I withhold forgiveness from others?

That doesn't mean forgiveness is easy. A significant wound is a loss that must be grieved . . . and grieving is hard! It's a process that requires prayer, time, surrender, and support. First, we need to understand what forgiveness is. In *The Reason for God*, Tim Keller explained,

Forgiveness means refusing to make them pay for what they did. However, to refrain from lashing out at someone when you want to do so with all your being is agony. It is a form of suffering. You not only suffer the original loss of happiness, reputation, and opportunity, but now you forgo the consolation of inflicting the same on them. You are absorbing the debt, taking the cost of it completely on yourself instead of taking it out of the other person. It hurts terribly. Many people would say it feels like a kind of death. Yes, but it is a death that leads to resurrection instead of the lifelong living death of bitterness and cynicism.[15]

But forgiveness is essential—not just for the person we're forgiving but for our own hearts. Holding onto anger and bitterness weighs us down while showing mercy sets us free.

For some of us, the person hardest to forgive is ourselves. We live under a dark cloud of shame, reliving our flaws, sins, and mistakes, and believing the solution is to feel bad enough long enough as some form of payment . . . but that never sets us free. Maybe you've made choices you regret, spoken words you wish you could take back, or carried guilt for years over something you can't undo. Jesus' words to the woman caught in adultery are words for you, too: "Neither do I condemn you. Go now and leave your life of sin." His mercy isn't just for the mistakes we make before we come to Him—it's for every stumble along the way. He doesn't hold our failures over us; He invites us to start fresh, walking in His grace.

Reflect and Pray

1. How do you think the woman felt when she was caught in the act of adultery and dragged before the religious leaders who wanted to stone her? Have you ever felt that way? If you have, what were the circumstances?

2. How is forgiveness different from excusing, minimizing, and denying what happened?

3. Look at Keller's quote again. How might it be helpful to realize forgiveness is "agony"?

4. Read Colossians 3:12-13. What's the connection between our experience of God's forgiveness and our ability to forgive others?

5. Ask God to give you a deeper grasp of His forgiveness for your sins so you'll have a greater ability to forgive those who hurt you.

DAY 5

Jesus Heals the Broken

**Then Jesus said to him, "Get up! Pick up your mat and walk."
At once the man was cured; he picked up his mat and walked.**

JOHN 5:8-9

THE STORY OF JESUS HEALING THE PARALYZED MAN at the pool of Bethesda is one of my favorite examples of His mercy. The man had been waiting for healing for thirty-eight long years. Can you imagine what that must have been like? I know many of our Extraordinary Women are younger than thirty-eight—the man had been waiting longer than they've been alive! Day after day, year after year, sitting by the water, hoping that today might be the day! The pool of Bethesda was believed to have healing properties, stirred by an angel at certain times. But for this man, even with the promise of healing so close, it always felt just out of reach.

Imagine the scene: a crowd of sick, disabled, and desperate people all clinging to hope. You can almost hear the hum of voices, the shuffling of people trying to get closer to the water, and the whispers of frustration from those who had waited too long. The paralyzed man, lying on his mat, must have felt the full weight of despair. He tells Jesus that he has no one to help him into the pool when the water is stirred, which speaks to a deep loneliness and helplessness. At that moment, when it felt like no one had seen him, Jesus did.

Jesus approached him—not to discuss theology or the myths about the pool, but to ask him one simple, profound question: "Do you want to get well?" At first glance, it seems like a very odd question. Of course, he wanted to get well! But it's easy to live with the familiar, even when it's painful and empty. Change requires courage, so it's easier to just stay stuck . . . and complain there's no hope. Our pain becomes such a part of us that the thought of healing feels impossible or even frightening. But Jesus' question was an invitation, cutting through the years of disappointment and offering a chance to hope again.

When Jesus told him, "Get up! Pick up your mat and walk," the man's life changed in an instant. He didn't need the pool; he needed Jesus' healing touch. At once, he was cured. The mat he had relied on for years was no longer a symbol of his helplessness but a testimony of his healing. Can you imagine the joy and wonder he must have felt as he stood steady on his feet for the first time in nearly four decades?

Bethesda means "house of mercy." What a fitting setting for this example of the power of God's mercy to meet us in our deepest need. It doesn't matter how long we've been waiting or how hopeless the situation seems—Jesus sees us. His mercy is not limited by time, circumstances, or our own doubts. He comes to us, not because we've earned it or proven ourselves worthy, but simply because He loves us.

At the end of this week, I'm encouraged that the Scriptures are real and raw about the struggles we face. In Psalm 73, the writer was full of resentment and self-pity because God hadn't come through for him like he expected. He describes his spiritual and emotional condition in a way that resonates with many of us:

> When my soul was embittered,
>   when I was pricked in heart,
> I was brutish and ignorant;
>   I was like a beast toward you.

Have you ever felt so angry, so disgusted, so disillusioned that you were like an animal? He did, so have we. But the psalm doesn't end there. A fresh insight filled his heart with gratitude:

> Nevertheless, I am continually with you;
>   you hold my right hand.
> You guide me with your counsel,
>   and afterward you will receive me to glory.
> Whom have I in heaven but you?
>   And there is nothing on earth that I desire besides you.

My flesh and my heart may fail,
    but God is the strength of my heart and my portion forever.
(Psalm 73:21-26)

Even when he was at his worst, God reached out to tenderly hold his hand. That's the image I want to leave with you this week.

If you're broken today, hear Jesus' question: "Do you want to get well?" It's an invitation to trust Him, to let go of what's holding you back, and to step into the life He has for you. Healing might not come instantly, but His presence is with you every step of the way.

Reflect and Pray

1. Read John 5:1-9. Describe the paralyzed man's situation and his long years of frustration.

2. How did Jesus' question cut through the man's passivity and complacency?

3. What are some reasons staying stuck feels safer than taking the risk of change?

4. Have you ever felt like a "beast" in your agony that life hasn't gone the way you expected? Describe what happened in the psalmist's heart that gave him relief and gratitude.

5. Ask God to warm your heart to His mercy, and ask Him to show you specific people and situations where you can be merciful to others.

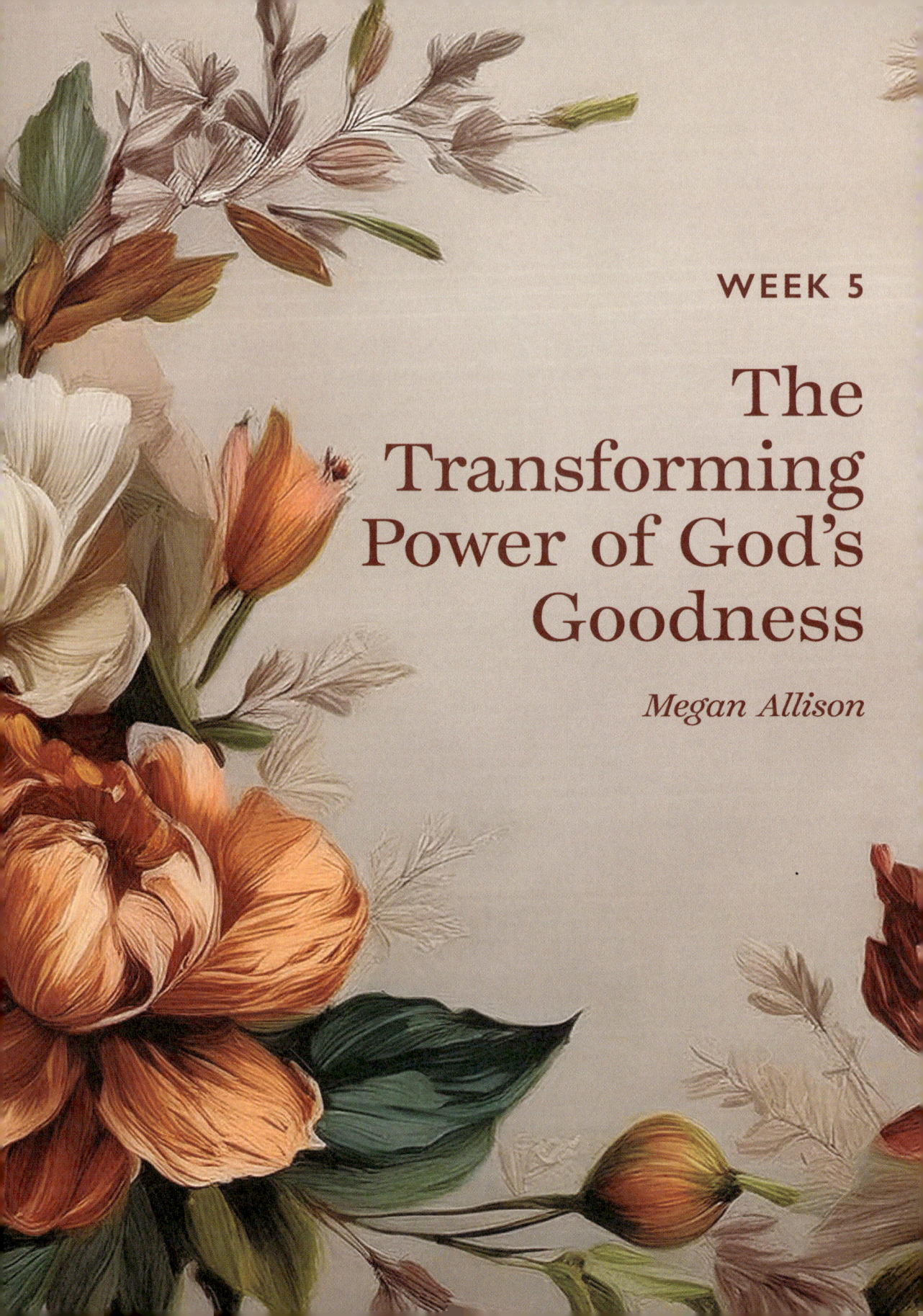

The Transforming Power of God's Goodness

Megan Allison

I RECENTLY WENT TO SIGHT AND SOUND THEATER in Lancaster, Pennsylvania, to see the play *Daniel*, and it was absolutely breathtaking. My husband, daughters, parents, brother Zach, and sister-in-law Evelyn went together during an Extraordinary Women conference weekend. From start to finish, the show was unforgettable.

For those who have never heard of Sight and Sound, the family-owned theater brings the Bible to life on stage. It started fifty years ago when a dairy farmer felt God's call to transition from farming to entertainment. The surprising career change was beyond successful, and now there are two locations, the one in Lancaster and another in Branson, Missouri. Both have the highest quality production and performance.

The production of *Daniel* was incredibly immersive. Real sheep were running up and down the aisles, and at one point, a towering, twenty-foot statue took my breath away. Olivia was completely captivated; she didn't move a muscle the entire show! The scene in the lions' den was especially memorable. The lions looked so real, yet not one of them touched Daniel. It was amazing to see God's protection brought to life so vividly. We make it a tradition to see a show there every year, but *Daniel* might be my favorite. The biblical rendition reminded me so much of my brother Zach's book, *Even If*, especially seeing Shadrach, Meshach, and Abednego stand firm in the fire—what a powerful display of faith!

In this week's devotions, we'll see how to overcome obstacles by trusting in God's goodness. Some of the situations we face are overwhelming, heartbreaking, or terrifying. This isn't an academic exercise for me. In my work, I sometimes need to share heartbreaking diagnoses with my patients, knowing that their next steps are going to be challenging. I pray that they find strength and peace through it all. Just as God was with Daniel in the lions' den, His goodness can carry us through the most frightening moments. When we trust in God's goodness during our hardest circumstances, we can find the courage to face whatever lies ahead.

Difficulties challenge our faith, but they also strengthen it. In a culture that promises instant answers and relief, nagging problems seem totally wrong . . . out of place . . . and confusing. The doctrine of God's goodness is encouraging, but the experience of His goodness carries us through our biggest challenges. Each day of our study this week, we'll see how His goodness is woven through Scripture, reminding us that we're never alone in our struggles.

We'll begin by reflecting on Christ's goodness through His example of humility and servant-hearted love. Washing the disciples' feet is a powerful picture of what it means to love others selflessly, even when it costs us something. We'll see how extending forgiveness enables us to overcome our self-pity and resentment and can pave the way to reconciliation. Forgiveness isn't just about letting go of past hurts—it's about stepping into freedom and trusting God to work all things for good. God's goodness is revealed in the many facets of how He protects us. He is our shield and strength. We'll see Jesus restore Peter after his big promise of loyalty and his cowardly denial. We'll end the week by grasping the peace that comes when our hearts are flooded with God's goodness.

As you move through these days of study, I pray that you'll find encouragement to overcome your challenges. Let's lean into the goodness of God and allow His love to transform our hearts and lives.

Overflowing with Christ's Goodness

"This is my commandment, that you love one another as I have loved you. Greater love has no one than this, that someone lay down his life for his friends."

JOHN 15:12-13

TODAY'S PASSAGE IS FOUND IN A SECTION of John's Gospel, chapters 13 through 17, often referred to as "the Farewell Discourse." Some theologians extend the section through chapter 20 and call it "the Book of Glory." As I dove into this portion of Scripture, I noted that the "Book of Glory" captures the days of the Last Supper, Jesus' instructions to His disciples, Judas's betrayal, the arrest and mock trial, Jesus' crucifixion, and His resurrection—all of it is focused on Jesus' ultimate act of love and sacrifice.

Jesus knew He was about to be betrayed and turned over to a kangaroo court, the innocent found guilty. He knew He would suffer excruciating physical pain, but even worse than that would be temporary separation from the Father. If I knew anything remotely similar to this trouble was coming, I'd be frantically trying to run from it! But Jesus, the Hero of heroes, poured out His love on those who followed Him (even though they were clueless about what was coming!).

Jesus shocked those sitting around the table during supper on that fateful night. He put His robe aside, picked up a towel and a water basin, and began washing the disciples' feet. This was a somewhat demeaning job typically assigned to the lowest-level house servant, but the King of Glory demonstrated stunning humility. Peter protests, "You shall never wash my feet" (John 13:8), until Jesus explains that this act is essential for their relationship. Remember, these guys had argued more than once about who would be the greatest in Christ's kingdom!

We often use the word "good" to refer to a pleasant event or tasty food, but in the Bible, the word means living for the benefit of others. God's goodness is His commitment to blessing us so that we can know Him more intimately and experience the wonder of His loving presence. In this event, Jesus demonstrated the depth of His commitment to His disciples and to us.

I'm sure this moment rang true for the disciples because Jesus had humbly cared for them countless times over the years they'd followed Him. But this was different. A few days earlier, Jesus had ridden into Jerusalem to the shouts of "Hosannah!" The disciples understood that Roman emperors and generals rode into cities they'd conquered and proclaimed themselves as masters. Isn't that what Jesus was doing? Wasn't He going to seize power and rule?

No, His kingdom (as He'd told them dozens of times) was very different from what they expected. He was going to rule through humility and sacrifice, as people's hearts were transformed by His love. Washing the disciples' feet was the polar opposite of what they expected! It wasn't merely a symbolic gesture or a ritual; it was a tangible expression of His goodness. By washing their feet, Jesus sets an example of what it means to truly love others—not just in words, but in action. His goodness is revealed not through grand displays of power but through acts of humility and service.

The disciples didn't comprehend the importance of humility in their relationships, and Jesus' example of service only confused them further. But do we do any better? In *Experiencing the Father's Embrace*, Pastor Jack Frost notes:

> The number one hindrance to an intimate walk with God, one in which we truly know and are truly known by Him, is the absence of humility. When we are more concerned with what other people think than with what God thinks of us—that is the absence of humility. When we justify our behavior, shift blame, accuse, find fault, criticize, or seek to vindicate ourselves—that is the absence of humility. When we had rather be right than have relationship—that is the absence of humility. When we do not confess our sins and our failures to others—that is the absence of humility. When we do not acknowledge our sins against love—that is the absence of humility. When we do not daily admit our desperate need for God to father us and help in our lives—that is the absence of humility.[16]

A few hours after washing the disciples' feet, as Jesus walked with them toward Gethsemane, He connected the dots: "My command is this: Love each other as I have loved you. Greater love has no one than this: to lay down one's life for one's friends" (John 15:12-13).

We can't give away something we don't possess, and we can't demonstrate a quality we haven't experienced. Notice the sequence: We can only love others to the extent we've experienced the love of God. What's the extent of Jesus' love for us? The cross. He laid down His life not just for the self-assured and mighty but for the broken, the hopeless, the confused, and the humble. These are the people who delight in being loved, and these are the people who are filled and overflow with His love toward others. That's the mark of God's goodness to us and our goodness to those around us.

As I reflect on this scene, I think about how we are called to reflect Christ's goodness in our lives. In my work, I've learned that even small acts of care can have a profound impact. Whether it's taking extra time to listen to a patient's concerns or offering a word of encouragement, I hope these moments mirror the love Jesus showed to His disciples . . . including me.

Jesus didn't just wash the feet of the disciples who would remain faithful. He washed Peter's feet, knowing he would deny Him. He washed Judas's feet, knowing Judas would betray Him. This is the radical goodness of Christ—a love that isn't contingent on us being perfect but is rooted in His incredible love.

When Jesus finished washing His disciples' feet, He told them, "Now that I, your Lord and Teacher, have washed your feet, you also should wash one another's feet" (John 13:14 NIV). This command isn't just about literal foot washing; it's about embracing a posture of humility and service in all we do. It's about loving others in a way that reflects Christ's sacrificial love, even when it's inconvenient, uncomfortable, or undeserved.

As we begin this week of devotionals, take a moment to reflect on how you can embody Christ's goodness. Who in your circle might need an act of kindness, a word of encouragement, or a helping hand? Remember, reflecting Christ's goodness isn't about being perfect—it's about choosing to love, serve, and give as He did. But maybe another question is more important: How deeply are you experiencing God's radical, limitless goodness?

Reflect and Pray

1. If the disciples expected Jesus to become a military commander, what do you imagine they were thinking when He got up to wash their feet?

2. Describe some differences between the power grab in the world's kingdoms (of politics and business) and the humility, grace, and love of Jesus' kingdom.

3. If we can't give away something we don't possess, what are some ways you can "possess" more of God's goodness? Will it be worth the effort? Explain your answer.

4. Who are some people that are hard for you to love? (Write in code!)

5. Ask God to amaze you with the depth of His love and goodness for you so these qualities become second nature.

Forgiving as We've Been Forgiven

**"I have set you an example that you should do
as I have done for you."**

JOHN 13:15

YES, WE LOOKED AT THE TOPIC OF FORGIVENESS last week, but most of us (all of us?) need continual reminders and at least a few fresh insights to help us become good at forgiving those who have wronged us. Forgiveness is one of the most challenging acts of love we're called to as Christians. It often feels impossible to extend grace when someone wrongs us, yet forgiveness is at the heart of God's goodness toward us. As I reflect on this, I'm reminded of how forgiveness not only restores relationships but also brings freedom and healing to our hearts. Forgiveness, though, requires understanding and courage.

Yesterday, we looked at Jesus washing the disciples' feet and saw that this gesture is an example for us to follow. Forgiveness is a constant theme in the Bible. Why? Because it's the key to experiencing God's magnificent grace, it deepens our gratitude, and it transforms our motivations.

The first three chapters of Paul's letter to the Ephesians are about our identity in Christ—how God's love is poured into us; the last three chapters are applications of our identity as chosen, adopted, forgiven children of God—how God's love pours from us into the lives of others. Paul gives several ethical directives: don't lie but speak the truth, don't steal but work hard, be angry but don't sin, and don't use poisonous words but let your speech give grace. But there's one more:

> And do not grieve the Holy Spirit of God, by whom you were sealed
> for the day of redemption. Let all bitterness and wrath and anger

and clamor and slander be put away from you, along with all malice. Be kind to one another, tenderhearted, forgiving one another, as God in Christ forgave you. Therefore be imitators of God, as beloved children. And walk in love, as Christ loved us and gave himself up for us, a fragrant offering and sacrifice to God. (Ephesians 4:30–5:2)

When people wrong us, our instinctual reaction is to run away, deny it happened, or get revenge (or all of these, at one time or another). Forgiving people requires a heart transformation. If we have difficulty forgiving someone, we don't just try harder. We dive deeper into the wonder of God forgiving us through Christ's payment for our sins. We might object, "But I haven't done what he (or she) did to me!" That's probably true, but our sins (perhaps self-righteousness) were so bad that it took the death of the Son of God to wash them away.

Jesus said to follow His example of washing feet, which is a symbol of forgiveness. And Paul encouraged us to become imitators of God—not through sheer willpower, but because we've received God's tenderness, kindness, compassion, and the care a "beloved" child receives from a loving parent.

Jesus commands us to love one another as He has loved us. This love isn't superficial or conditional; it's sacrificial and boundless. It's the kind of love that led Jesus to the cross to bear the weight of our sins. Through His death and resurrection, He showed us what it means to forgive completely and to release others from the debt they owe us, just as God has released us from ours.

Forgiving someone who has hurt us is no small task. I've struggled with this myself. Whether it's the sting of a harsh word or a deeper betrayal, my first instinct isn't tenderness and love! But I've learned that forgiveness isn't about denying the hurt or pretending everything is okay. It's about reflecting God's goodness by grieving the loss and releasing the anger, resentment, and desire for revenge.

Writer and theologian Lewis Smedes has observed: "Forgiving does not erase the bitter past. A healed memory is not a deleted memory. Instead, forgiving what we cannot forget creates a new way to remember. We change the memory of our past into a hope for our future."[17]

When we forgive, we overcome the bitterness that can take root in our hearts. We overcome the mistaken belief that holding a grudge gives us power or control. We trust God to be just, so we don't have to punish the offender. He will bring justice and healing in His time so we can surrender our desire for revenge.

Of course, we're not always the ones who were wronged; we hurt others in many different ways. We confess to God when we've sinned against Him, and we confess to others when we've hurt them.

Joseph forgave his brothers for selling him into slavery. Despite their betrayal, Joseph chose to see God's hand in his circumstances, telling them, "You intended to harm me, but God intended it for good to accomplish what is now being done, the saving of many lives" (Genesis 50:20). Joseph's forgiveness didn't erase the pain of his past. Still, it allowed him to step into God's greater purpose for his life.

I see forgiveness play out in small but meaningful ways with my daughters, Olivia and Sophia. Whether it's sharing toys or mending hurt feelings after an argument, their moments of reconciliation remind me of the simple yet profound truth that forgiveness restores joy and peace. If a five-year-old can say, "I'm sorry" and hug her sister, surely we can ask God to help us forgive those who have wronged us.

Our capacity to forgive others is a reflection of the forgiveness we've received from God. When we grieve the hurt and extend grace, we're living out the gospel in a tangible way. And through this, we show the world what it means to follow Christ—a life marked by love, mercy, and goodness.

When I read a study like this or hear a speaker talk about forgiveness, God usually taps me on the shoulder to say, "Dear daughter, you haven't dealt with this offense yet. It's time." Maybe the Lord is tapping you on the shoulder right now. Consider who you might need to forgive. Ask God to give you the strength to release the burden, trusting Him to give you strength. Remember, forgiveness isn't a one-time event; it's a journey. And as we forgive, we draw closer to God's goodness and reflect His love to those around us.

Reflect and Pray

1. What are some reasons forgiving others is so hard?

2. Look at the Ephesians passage we studied today. Describe the motivation to imitate God by forgiving those who offend us.

3. Reflect on Genesis 50:20. How does Joseph's perspective on forgiveness inspire you to trust God's purpose in difficult situations?

4. Are there any "loose ends" of forgiveness or confession in your life? (For most of us, the answer is yes!) Who has come to mind as you've studied today's lesson? What is your first step?

5. Ask God to give you a clear plan and the courage to move forward to forgive and ask for forgiveness.

DAY 3

The Goodness of God's Protection

"My prayer is not that you take them out of the world but that you protect them from the evil one. They are not of the world, even as I am not of it. Sanctify them by the truth; your word is truth."

JOHN 17:15-17, NIV

One of my greatest desires is to protect my daughters from harm. Whether Sophia is learning to navigate the playground or Olivia is venturing into new friendships at school, my instinct is to shield them from any difficulties they might face. But in reality, I can't remove all challenges from their lives, yet I can teach them to face those challenges with confidence, knowing they are loved and protected.

In today's Scripture, Jesus prays not for His followers to be taken out of the world but instead asks for their protection while they remain in it. This passage reminds me of the Lord's Prayer, where we ask God to "deliver us from the evil one" (Matthew 6:13). Jesus acknowledges the reality of evil in this world—the pain, the sorrow, the spiritual battles we face—and yet He assures us of His presence and protection. He doesn't promise a life free from hardship, but He promises to walk with us through any difficulty we face.

One of the most comforting truths in these verses is that Jesus is our defense. Satan may try to harm our bodies, create fear, or sow discouragement, but he can never touch the eternal security of our souls. Jesus' prayer reminds us that we are under His divine care, even in the midst of life's storms. He shields us with His truth, guiding and strengthening us to resist the schemes of the evil one.

This passage reminds me of the forty days Jesus was tempted in the wilderness just after His baptism. In Luke's account, Satan first used Jesus' hunger to tempt Him with food.

Then, he promised Jesus a kingdom on earth without having to go to the cross. Finally, Satan used passages from the Bible to try to trick Jesus, but He would have nothing of it. Each time, Jesus responded with the right interpretation and application of the Word of God.

God's truth reveals His strong and loving character, describes the nature of grace and salvation, and points us to choices that honor God. But God's truth also reminds us that what we see around us each day isn't all there is. An unseen world surrounds us. We have only a limited grasp of the spiritual conflict going on, but we have God's Word to comfort and guide. To "sanctify" means to set apart. The "truth" shows us what it means to be a faithful servant of God in a fallen world. We are not *of* the world, but we are *in* the world, and we are *for* the world.

This truth has been especially meaningful to me in my work. Just as Jesus prays for us to be sanctified by the truth of His Word, I encourage my patients to anchor themselves in hope and trust during their trials.

It may be difficult for some of us to grasp, but Jesus delights in us. When we testify to His goodness and share how His protection has carried us through, we glorify Him and strengthen others. It's easy to focus on our struggles, but remembering to celebrate God's faithfulness shifts our perspective and renews our courage.

Take a moment to reflect on how Jesus has protected you in the past. Maybe it was a moment when He gave you strength to resist temptation, peace in the midst of fear, or renewed hope during a season of sorrow. Whatever it was, hold onto that memory as a reminder that He is with you now and always. Let His prayer in John 17 encourage you to trust in the goodness of His protection.

Reflect and Pray

1. Remember times when God gave you wisdom and strength to avoid giving in to temptation. What difference did His protection make for you?

2. When you're in a battle or facing temptation, has God's protection ever failed? Why or why not?

3. What does it mean to you to be "in the world, but not of the world, and for the world"? What are some practical applications of each part of this statement?

4. What's the role of the truth of God's Word in protecting us?

5. Ask God to deepen your trust in Him as you face temptation, trials, and difficulties.

DAY 4

The Goodness of Redemption

[Jesus] said to him the third time, "Simon, son of John, do
you love me?" Peter was grieved because he said to him the
third time, "Do you love me?" and he said to him,
"Lord, you know everything; you know that I love you."
Jesus said to him, "Feed my sheep."

(JOHN 21:15-17)

HAVE YOU EVER HAD A MOMENT WHEN YOU KNEW you'd let someone down? I know many moms feel this acutely on the tough days—like when we are so tired after a long day at work or when we get so caught up in our to-do lists that we aren't paying attention to a little one talking to us. Those moments can leave us feeling guilty, but they also remind us that God's mercy is bigger than our failures, big and small.

Peter knew he had let Jesus down. At dinner earlier that night, he had made a grand pronouncement that he was willing to die for Jesus, and when Jesus was being arrested, Peter impulsively swung a sword and cut off the ear of the high priest's servant. Jesus healed the wound, replacing the ear (and I can almost see Him shake His head and mutter, "Oh Peter . . .").

As Jesus was interrogated, Peter listened near the door. When a servant girl suggested he had been with Jesus, he denied it. (Notice that he perceived a threat from a young girl, not a Roman soldier!) Then, two others asked if he was a disciple of Jesus, and Peter erupted, "Man, I do not know what you are talking about" (Luke 22:60). At that moment, a rooster crowed. Peter was shattered with shame and "went out and wept bitterly" (vs. 62).

Was it over for Peter? Could he face Jesus again?

Peter was in the Upper Room the night after the resurrection when Jesus appeared to them, but we don't read about any interaction between them. I'm sure the shame stuck to him like glue. I imagine him replaying those moments in his mind, wondering if he could ever be trusted again. But then, on the shore of the Sea of Galilee, Jesus offers him a second chance.

Peter and some other disciples had been fishing all night but caught nothing. At dawn, they noticed someone on the beach who told them to lower their nets. They caught a lot of huge fish, which I'm sure reminded Peter of the enormous catch when Jesus first called him to follow Him. Peter jumped into the water and swam to shore. There, Jesus had built a charcoal fire. This detail is important because it's the same kind of fire by which Peter warmed himself as he listened to Jesus' first trial and denied Him three times. The smell of the fire on the beach reminded him of the depth of his sin—no rationalizing, no minimizing, no excusing. Jesus had orchestrated the moment so Peter had to face the hard facts.

But Jesus wasn't being unkind. He wanted the restoration to reach into the deepest recesses of Peter's heart. Jesus asked him, "Do you love me?"—not once, but three times. In the first two questions, Peter responds, "Yes, Lord; you know that I love you." When Jesus asks a third time, Peter realized this was the way to face his greatest failure and deepest shame. He was deeply saddened, but he replied, "Lord, you know everything; you know that I love you" (John 21:15-17). By asking Peter this question, Jesus is inviting him to reaffirm his devotion. He is calling him to a greater level of love and commitment.

Each time Peter affirms his love, Jesus responds with commands: "Feed my lambs," "Tend my sheep," and "Feed my sheep." This isn't just a directive to care for others—it's a reinstatement of Peter's purpose. Despite his failures, Jesus entrusts Peter with the responsibility of leading and nurturing the Christian community. What grace! Jesus doesn't dwell on Peter's past; instead, He calls him into a future of faithfulness and service.

This story reminds us that failure doesn't disqualify us from God's plans. In fact, He often uses our brokenness to deepen our dependence on Him and prepare us for greater things. Like Peter, we're called to demonstrate our love for Jesus through action—by serving others, extending grace, and living out His love in our daily lives.

If you've ever felt like your failures have sidelined you, hear this: Jesus isn't finished with you. Just as He restored Peter, He wants to restore you. He doesn't ask for perfection—He asks for love. This moment for Peter was undoubtedly painful at first, but it led to a fresh wind of forgiveness, restoration, joy, and purpose.

Are you haunted by failures? Take some time to reflect on Jesus' question: "Do you love me?" Let His mercy draw you into a deeper relationship with Him, and let His goodness and grace remind you that your story isn't over. There is still work to be done, and He is calling you to feed His sheep.

Reflect and Pray

1. Describe what you think was going on in Peter's mind and heart when he heard the rooster crow and wept bitter tears.

2. How does being haunted by failures affect us spiritually, mentally, emotionally, relationally, and physically?

3. Put yourself in this story and imagine the charcoal fire, being called by Jesus for a private conversation, and hearing three times, "Do you love me?" What would you be thinking and feeling? At the end of the conversation, would your perspective and emotions be changed? Why or why not?

4. What are practical ways you can feed Jesus' sheep? Which of these is most meaningful to you? Explain your answer.

5. Ask God to remind you of the depth of His forgiveness and the joy of restoration.

Resting in His Goodness

**"Peace I leave with you; my peace I give to you.
Not as the world gives do I give to you. Let not your hearts
be troubled, neither let them be afraid."**

JOHN 14:27

"Rest" isn't something moms get a lot of. I often joke that my younger daughter, Sophia Diane, is my "Velcro child" because she likes to stick to me. Even as she's growing older, her needs are still constant—though they change with each stage—and some days it feels like sleep is a distant memory for me. Sophia didn't sleep through the night until she was thirteen months old. Thirteen months! For over a year, I ran on coffee, prayers, and grace. But in that season of exhaustion, I learned something profound about rest: it's about so much more than sleep.

True rest comes when we trust. It's easy to think that rest is something we earn, like a reward for getting everything done or holding it all together. The kind of peace the world promises is fickle and fleeting. It's based on finally finding rest when we've accomplished a big task or avoided a responsibility. But Jesus offers a different kind of rest. He invites us to lay down our striving and lean into His goodness and mercy. In John 14:27, He promises a peace that is unlike anything the world can offer—a peace that steadies our hearts and quiets our fears. This peace doesn't depend on perfect circumstances or a full night's sleep; it comes from knowing that He is with us and for us.

To help me embrace this kind of rest, I've reframed it as an acronym:

> » R – Rely on and remember the truth of God's promises.
>
> Scriptures like John 3:16 and Proverbs 3:5-6 remind us that God's love is unchanging and His guidance is sure. Resting in His mercy starts with trusting that He keeps His promises.

» E – Enjoy the little moments.

Psalm 118:24 says, "This is the day the Lord has made; let us rejoice and be glad in it." Resting isn't just about stopping; it's about being fully present. Whether it's interacting with patients, strategizing with Ben, cuddling with Sophia, listening to Olivia's latest kindergarten adventure, or watching the sunset, these moments remind me of God's goodness.

» S – Surround yourself with uplifting people.

The Bible tells us, "As iron sharpens iron, so one person sharpens another" (Proverbs 27:17). Who we spend time with matters. Surrounding myself with friends and family who encourage me helps me find rest even in busy seasons.

» T – Be thankful.

Gratitude shifts our perspective. Taking time to express thanks to God for His mercy and provision—especially on the hard days—reminds us that He is our source of strength and joy.

Rest isn't about perfection or productivity. It's about leaning into God's goodness and trusting that He is enough for whatever comes our way. As moms, women, and believers, we will have seasons when life feels overwhelming, but His mercy never runs out. When we rely on His promises, enjoy His gifts, surround ourselves with support, and practice thankfulness, we experience a deeper kind of rest—one that sustains us in every season.

Today, take a moment to breathe. Let go of the burdens you're carrying, and hear Jesus' invitation: "Come to me, all you who are weary and burdened, and I will give you rest" (Matthew 11:28). His rest is yours to receive.

Reflect and Pray

1. What kind of rest does the world offer? What are some reasons it's not satisfying for long?

2. Which part of the REST acronym (Rely, Enjoy, Surround, Thanks) do you feel drawn to today? Why?

3. Is it possible to be busy but still have a heart at rest? If so, what has to happen for it to be realized?

4. What are some ways the discipline of gratitude shifts our perspective?

5. Ask God to help you take bold, clear steps to lean on Him so you can experience true rest.

WEEK 6

Receiving Mercy in Time of Weakness

Megan Allison

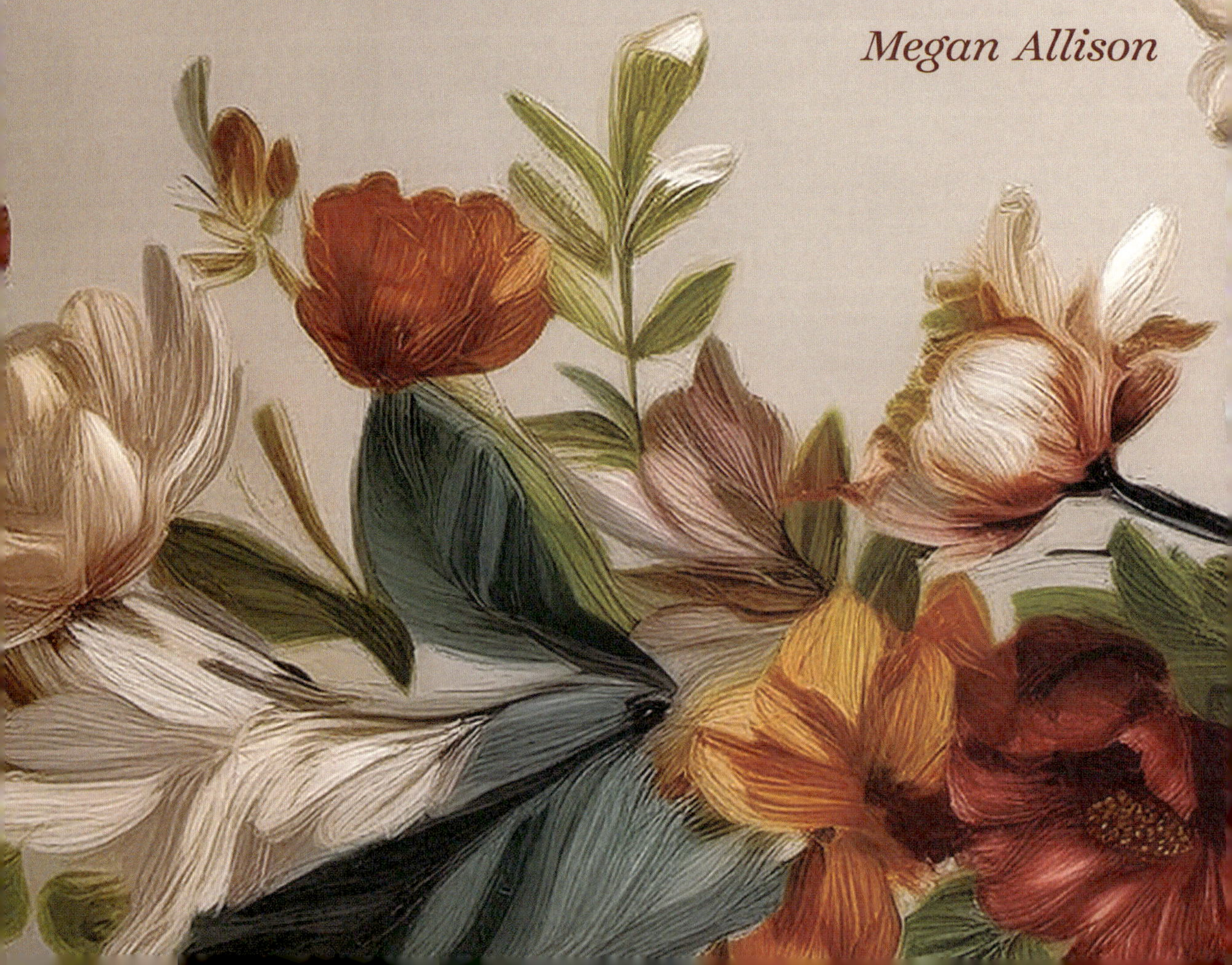

HAVE YOU EVER FELT LIKE YOU'VE FALLEN SHORT—whether in your relationships, your faith, or just in the day-to-day challenges of life? I know I've had moments where I've felt weak, inadequate, and in need of God's mercy. This week, we're going to explore how God meets us in those moments with His compassion and strength. We'll spend a couple of days looking at the consolation offered in Isaiah, and then the rest of the week we'll dig deep into the book of Hebrews, a letter filled with truths about Jesus and His role as our merciful high priest.

Hebrews stands out to me as one of the Bible's most theologically deep and Christ-centered books. It was written to early Christians who had heard the gospel from those who were eyewitnesses of Christ (Hebrews 2:3). They were not new to the faith (5:12), but they had become "dull of hearing" (5:11) and were in danger of drifting away from their commitment to Jesus. Hebrews is a call to return to Him, to hold firmly to faith, and to embrace the grace and mercy He offers in our weaknesses. How applicable today to read the call to hold firmly to our faith in Jesus!

When we study this book, it helps to know that Hebrews can be divided into five main sections: chapters 1 and 2 compare Jesus to the angels and the Torah; chapters 3 and 4 compare Him to Moses and the promised land; chapters 5 through 7 reveal Jesus as the ultimate High Priest; chapters 8 through 10 focus on His once-for-all sacrifice and the new covenant; and chapters 11 through 13 challenge us to follow Jesus no matter the cost. Some think that Hebrews was written by the Apostle Paul, while other possibilities include Apollos, Priscilla, Aquila, Luke, Barnabas, or an anonymous Jewish Christian.

Another thing I love about Hebrews is its many connections to the Old Testament. You can find nearly 100 references to Old Testament Scriptures, especially from the Septuagint (the earliest known Greek translation of the Old Testament). As you read through Hebrews, watch for words like *better*, *heavenly*, *perfect*, and *by faith*. These words describe the surpassing greatness of Jesus and the hope we have in Him.

This week, we will explore how God's mercy meets us in our weaknesses. On Day 1, we'll reflect on trusting God's presence, drawing from Isaiah's reminder to not fear because God is with us. Day 2 will focus on God's strength and His promise to renew and lift us up like eagles. On Day 3, we'll see Jesus as a merciful high priest who empathizes with our struggles. Day 4 is an affirmation of how God's grace is sufficient in our weaknesses and always available when we boldly approach the throne of grace to find help in our time of need. Finally, on Day 5, we'll reflect on the cleansing power of confession after drawing near to God with hearts made pure by His mercy.

As we walk through these Scriptures together, my mom and I pray your hope and strength will be renewed. Whether you're facing struggles, doubts, or the weight of your imperfections, God's mercy is always available. Let's lean into His love and let Him meet us where we are, turning our weaknesses into an opportunity for His power to shine.

Trusting in God's Presence

**"Fear not, for I am with you; do not be dismayed,
for I am your God. I will strengthen you, I will help you,
I will uphold you with my righteous right hand."**

ISAIAH 41:10

ISAIAH 41:10 IS ONE OF THOSE VERSES that can warm you like a fireplace on a cold, rainy day. Its words can carry you through sleepless nights, seasons of uncertainty, and moments when you feel completely overwhelmed. God's promises in this verse are personal, powerful, and exactly what we need when we feel the weight of fear pressing in.

The context of this chapter is fascinating. God is speaking to Israel, His chosen people, who were facing exile and oppression. He assures them of His presence, strength, and help, saying, "Fear not, for I am with you." The imagery here is beautiful. God is not distant or indifferent; He is close, tenderly upholding His people. He speaks as a Redeemer who understands their weakness and promises to meet them in it.

The first promise in Isaiah 41:10 is God's presence: "I am with you." This assurance is the true antidote to fear. Fear thrives in isolation, and it whispers lies like, "You're alone in this," or "There's no way out." But when we are faithful to read and apply God's words, they cut through the noise. "I am with you" means that God isn't just nearby; He's actively involved, walking beside us through every challenge, and upholding us!

The awareness of God's presence changes everything. When Olivia or Sophia face a tough moment—whether it's trying something new or dealing with a hurt—I always tell them, "Mommy's right here." Just knowing they're not alone gives them courage. If my presence as a human mom can bring comfort, how much more can the presence of our heavenly Father calm our hearts?

Another promise in this verse is God's power. He promises to strengthen, help, and uphold us. This is personal and intentional help—God doesn't just empower us and then leave us to figure things out on our own. He walks with us, holding us steady when we feel like we're about to fall.

This promise reminds me of how God's people were often described as weak and vulnerable, even compared to a "worm" in Isaiah 41:14. If you wonder why God would call His people a *worm*, it does make sense in this case because worms are powerless and lowly. However, the specific worm referred to here was from an insect used to make scarlet dye. Biblically, scarlet symbolizes sacrifice—and as ladies who study God's Word, we know that the Redeemer mentioned later in that verse would make a great sacrifice for His people. And even though God acknowledges His people's frailty, He never dismisses or shames them. The same God who created the universe holds our right hand, guiding us, steadying us, and lifting us when we feel crushed under the weight of life.

In moments of fear, it's easy to focus on the size of our problems instead of the greatness of our God. This becomes a habit for some people. Max Lucado has noted: "You know people just assume, 'Well, all my life I'll be a worrier.' That doesn't have to be true. There's a way to drink from God's Presence so much that worry begins to dissipate."[18]

Instead of always reverting to fear and anxiety, we need to shift our perspective. God's righteous right hand—a symbol of His power, justice, and faithfulness—upholds us. When we feel unsteady, His strength is enough to carry us through. Our God has cared for His people, has sent His son, and in His goodness and mercy has made salvation and protection available to us all. When we feel afraid, overwhelmed, or weak, God's presence and strength are our firm foundation. He doesn't promise a life free from challenges, but He does promise to be with us in every step, providing exactly what we need to stand firm.

Reflect and Pray

1. Recall a time when you felt God's presence in the midst of fear. How did it give you courage?

2. Read Isaiah 41:8-20 to get more context. What promise in this passage stands out most to you today?

3. How does knowing that God holds your right hand (Isaiah 41:13) change your perspective on your current struggles?

4. The next time you're on the verge of panic, what can you do to remind yourself that God has promised, "I am with you"?

5. Read Psalm 22, a song that Jesus quoted from on the cross. What complaints of the psalmist can you relate to? What positive statements does he make that encourage you? Turn this Psalm into a prayer by paraphrasing it.

God's Strength in Our Lives

**He gives power to the faint, and to him who has no might
he increases strength. Even youths shall faint and be weary,
and young men shall fall exhausted; but they who wait for
the Lord shall renew their strength; they shall mount up with
wings like eagles; they shall run and not be weary;
they shall walk and not faint.**

ISAIAH 40:29-31

THE ABOVE PASSAGE CONCLUDES THE CHAPTER of Isaiah that begins with the words, *"Comfort, comfort my people,"* and then unfolds as a declaration of God's unmatched greatness, power, and care. These verses remind us that we serve a God who, unlike us, does not grow tired, does not faint, and is always a source of strength and renewal.

The context of Isaiah 40 is significant. God's people were either in or approaching exile, facing what must have felt like insurmountable challenges. It's hard to imagine a bleaker circumstance. Their land, their temple, and their sense of identity had been taken from them. Yet it was in this place of deep despair that God spoke through Isaiah, reminding them that His power and promises are unshakable. Just as He would deliver them from Babylon, He would also strengthen and uphold them in the midst of their trials.

The imagery in the closing verses is powerful. Human strength is limited, so even the strongest among us—"youths" and "young men"—will inevitably grow weary and fall. No matter how capable we are, a moment always comes when our resources run out. But this is exactly where God meets us. He doesn't scold us for our weakness or tell us to try harder. Instead, He gives strength to the weary and increases power to the weak.

Even though Isaiah uses a male pronoun, I am certain that most moms feel this truth deeply. New moms have days when they feel like their legs can't take one more step—learning to meet a newborn baby's needs on little sleep is simply overwhelming! Older moms lose sleep many nights while praying over their *parents'* health, but when morning arrives, they must get started on their day no matter how physically weak they feel. It's during those challenging (difficult!) times when we need to turn to God to find the strength to keep going. Personally, I've seen God provide clarity many times when my mind felt clouded. He has supplied energy when I felt drained, and hope when I felt discouraged.

God's strength isn't just a vague idea; it's a tangible reality. Pastor and author Paul David Tripp reminds us, "Remember, it is not your weakness that will get in the way of God's working through you, but your delusions of strength. His strength is made perfect in our weakness! Point to His strength by being willing to admit your weakness."[19]

God lifts us up when we're feeling feeble, holds us steady when we're about to fall, and equips us to face what's ahead. His strength is perfect, not just because it's limitless, but because it meets us exactly where we are, in exactly the way we need.

However, the promise of renewed strength comes with a condition: it comes to "those who wait for [hope in] the Lord." To wait for the Lord is not a passive resignation but an active trust in His timing and provision. It's a confident expectation that He will come through, even when we don't see immediate results.

The word *renew* in this passage carries a sense of exchanging our weakness for God's strength. This isn't a temporary boost of energy; it's a divine exchange where God gives us His power in place of our limitations. Matthew Strong's commentary reflects on this beautifully, noting that God's grace is "sufficient for every task He calls us to, whether it's soaring upward like eagles, running with perseverance, or walking faithfully through the day-to-day challenges."

I've always loved the progression in that last verse of Isaiah 40: soaring like eagles, running without growing weary, and walking without becoming faint. It shows that God's strength equips us for every season of life. Sometimes we're soaring, filled with inspiration and purpose. Other times, we're running, persevering through busy and demanding seasons. And then there are the days when all we can do is walk—but even then, God promises to sustain us.

Today's passage invites us to exchange our striving for resting in God's strength. It reminds us that even in our weariness, we are never alone. God's power is made perfect in our weakness, and His grace is always sufficient.

Reflect and Pray

1. Reread Isaiah 40:29-31, the verses that begin today's devotional. What does it mean to you that God gives strength to the weary?

2. How does waiting for the Lord encourage you in your current season? How does it challenge you?

3. Reflect on a time when you experienced God's strength in the midst of your weakness. Describe the situation and how it was resolved.

4. God once told the Apostle Paul, "My grace is sufficient for you, for my power is made perfect in weakness" (2 Corinthians 12:9). How does this statement deepen your understanding of the Isaiah passage?

5. In what ways can you actively wait for the Lord this week, trusting Him to renew your strength? Ask God to help you wait with patience and faith.

Jesus, Our Merciful High Priest

[Jesus] had to be made like his brothers in every respect, so that he might become a merciful and faithful high priest in the service of God, to make propitiation for the sins of the people. For because he himself has suffered when tempted, he is able to help those who are being tempted.

HEBREWS 2:17-18

Jesus as our high priest is not a role we may think about often—at least, I know that for many years, I didn't! For most Christian denominations, *priest* isn't even an often-used term unless we happen to be studying the Old Testament. However, because it is used in Scripture to describe our Savior, it's worth digging into and learning about. So, let's dig in!

The role of the high priest in the Old Testament was central to Israel's relationship with God. A priest acted as a mediator, offering sacrifices to atone for the sins of the people. Yet the old covenant system was temporary, pointing forward to something greater—a perfect and eternal solution. Hebrews identifies Jesus as that solution (4:14).

Today's passage reminds us that Jesus (who was both fully human and fully divine) became like us so that He could represent us before God. He not only understands our struggles, but He also made a way for us to approach God with confidence, knowing that our sins are fully atoned for.

Jesus' humanity is essential to His role as high priest. Without becoming fully human, He couldn't effectively identify with our weaknesses or serve as our representative before God. His incarnation was necessary for Him to bear our sins and make reconciliation possible.

Jesus faced every human experience—birth, hunger, exhaustion, joy, sorrow, temptation, and even death—all while remaining sinless (Hebrews 4:15). His sinlessness is what makes Him the perfect mediator and sacrifice. He was not only willing but also able to stand in our place, taking the punishment we deserved.

In His humanity, Jesus understands our pain and struggles, but as God, He has the power to save us. This dual nature is the cornerstone of our faith and the foundation of our hope.

The role of the high priest was to mediate between God and humanity, offering sacrifices for sin. But the priests of the old covenant were far from sinless—they had to offer sacrifices not only for the people but also for themselves (Hebrews 7:27). They served in an earthly tabernacle, a copy of the true heavenly reality (Hebrews 8:5). Jesus, however, is the perfect high priest, surpassing all who came before Him.

Here are some truths about Jesus that we can glean from the book of Hebrews. As you study these truths, you may want to refer to the sections of Hebrews that were listed in this week's introduction.

1. Jesus is both merciful and faithful (Hebrews 2:17).

> » His mercy flows from His compassion for humanity, as He fully understands our weaknesses and needs.
>
> » His faithfulness ensures that He fulfills every promise of God, mediating on our behalf with unwavering commitment.

2. Jesus offered himself as the ultimate sacrifice (Hebrews 9:12; 10:10).

> » Unlike the old covenant priests who repeatedly offered animal sacrifices, Jesus offered His own blood, once for all, securing eternal redemption. This sacrifice was perfect and sufficient, fully satisfying the demands of God's justice.

3. Jesus continually intercedes for us (Hebrews 7:25).

> » His priesthood is eternal, meaning His work of intercession never ceases.
>
> » Right now, Jesus is at the right hand of the Father, advocating for us and ensuring our access to God.

4. Jesus' sacrifice brought us under a new covenant (Hebrews 8:6-13).

   » Under this covenant, God writes His laws on our hearts, forgives our sins, and remembers them no more.

5. Jesus empathizes with our struggles (Hebrews 4:15).

   » He knows what it means to be tempted and weak, yet His victory over sin gives us confidence to approach Him for help.

Jesus, our merciful high priest, stands ready to help us in every trial. His atoning work on the cross and His ongoing intercession provide the foundation for our faith and the strength to face life's challenges. Take time today to reflect on His mercy and faithfulness. Whatever you're struggling with, bring it to Him, trusting that He understands and is able to help.

Reflect and Pray

1. Reflect on Hebrews 2:17-18. How does Jesus' humanity deepen your understanding of His mercy?

2. Reflect on Hebrews 9:12 and 10:10. How does Jesus' sacrifice provide confidence in your salvation?

3. In what ways do you need Jesus' intercession today? How does Hebrews 7:25 encourage you?

4. In Romans 5:10, Paul echoes these passages in Hebrews as he writes, "For if while we were enemies we were reconciled to God by the death of his Son, much more, now that we are reconciled, shall we be saved by his life." How does Jesus' role as our reconciler affect the way you approach God?

5. How can you share the hope of Jesus' mercy and faithfulness with someone this week? Ask God to put someone on your heart and direct your path.

Grace in Weakness

For we do not have a high priest who is unable to empathize with our weaknesses, but one who in every respect has been tempted as we are, yet without sin. Let us then with confidence draw near to the throne of grace, that we may receive mercy and find grace to help in time of need.

HEBREWS 4:15-16

Isn't it so nice when you meet someone who truly understands you? A few years ago, my brother, Zach, married a sweet girl named Evelyn, and we got to add another female to our family. Only those of you who grew up with brothers and then got sisters later in life can know my excitement! Evelyn has blessed our family in so many ways, and God gave me an extra blessing when He sent me a sister-in-law who is also in the medical field! Evelyn is a nurturing and friendly soul. She had already grown up with four close sisters (she's a triplet with two of them!), so I was quite touched by her genuine excitement in connecting with me.

Evelyn grew up in California, went to a private school just like I did, and always loved the medical field. Now, we both practice in Virginia where we've formed a special bond. We recently attended a dermatology conference together in Florida. The whole family joined us, and sometimes we all went to amusement parks together. Other times, the rest of the family enjoyed vacation time while Evelyn and I went to conference sessions—and it was tremendous joy to have a close friend with whom I share so many interests.

As humbling as it is to think, Jesus can be a special friend with us because He came to earth, took on human form, and went through all the human challenges that we do. He understands our struggles in a personal way. We don't have to fear God and tremble before Him every time we make a mistake. As we saw yesterday, Old Testament priests served as mediators between God and the people, offering sacrifices for their sins. But Jesus surpasses every earthly priest because He doesn't merely offer a sacrifice; He *is* the sacrifice. He's the perfect sacrifice because "he committed no sin, neither was deceit found in his mouth" (1 Peter 2:22). Yet when He intercedes for us before God, He fully understands what it means to be human. In addition, the writer of Hebrews also tells us:

> The former priests were many in number, because they were prevented by death from continuing in office, but [Jesus] holds his priesthood permanently, because he continues forever. Consequently, he is able to save to the uttermost those who draw near to God through him, since he always lives to make intercession for them. (Hebrews 7:23-25)

Empathy is a powerful thing. Today's Scripture assures us that Jesus is not a distant figure, untouched by the realities of human life. Instead, He entered fully into our experience, shared in our humanity, and now walks with us through our struggles. When a friend truly understands what you're going through, it brings a sense of comfort and relief, but Jesus' empathy goes even deeper because it's combined with His divine power. He doesn't just understand; He is able to help us overcome.

Consider how His empathy transforms our relationship with Him. Because He understands, we don't have to hide our struggles or put up a façade of strength. We can come to Him just as we are, confident that He will meet us with grace. His invitation in Hebrews 4:16 is clear: we can approach God's throne of grace with confidence.

The phrase *throne of grace* is meaningful. A throne often symbolizes authority, power, and judgment. But God's throne is described as a place of grace—where mercy and help are freely given. The God we serve welcomes us into His presence, not with condemnation but with open arms.

However, approaching God with confidence doesn't give us the right to be arrogant. It means we come with trust. We humbly believe that Jesus' sacrifice has made a way for us to stand before a holy God without fear.

In moments of weakness, this truth is our anchor. When we're tempted, we can turn to Jesus for strength. When we fail, we can turn to Him for forgiveness. When we're discouraged, we can turn to Him for hope. Every time we approach His throne, we're reminded that His grace is sufficient and His love is unchanging.

Jesus, our perfect high priest, has made a way for us to come boldly into God's presence, confident that we'll receive mercy and forgiveness in our time of need. His invitation to approach God's throne of grace is one of the most beautiful gifts we have as believers.

Reflect and Pray

1. How does Jesus' empathy make Him a superior high priest?

2. Reflect on Hebrews 7:23-25. What does it mean to you that Jesus is always interceding for you?

3. How does the imagery of God's "throne of grace" affect your understanding of prayer?

4. Reflect on 1 Peter 2:22. How does Jesus' sinlessness give you confidence in His ability to help you?

5. Take a moment today to reflect on your weaknesses. Where do you need Jesus' help? What burdens are you carrying that you can bring to Him? Trust that He understands and is ready to meet you with compassion, strength, and grace.

Confession and Cleansing

Since we have a great priest over the house of God, let us draw near with a true heart in full assurance of faith, with our hearts sprinkled clean from an evil conscience and our bodies washed with pure water. Let us hold fast the confession of our hope without wavering, for he who promised is faithful.

HEBREWS 10:21-23

WE'VE ALL EXPERIENCED MOMENTS where the weight of our mistakes feels overwhelming, where guilt whispers that we are unworthy of drawing near to God. But Hebrews 10:21-23 reminds us of a beautiful truth: we are invited to come into God's presence, not because of anything we've done, but because of what Jesus has done for us. His sacrifice has made a way for us to approach God with confidence, fully assured of His love and mercy.

This passage speaks to two key actions for believers: confession and cleansing. Some people tend to have a negative reaction when they hear the word *confession*. How many police dramas have you seen where a suspect is taken into a dingy, poorly lighted interrogation room where a detective or two attempts to "sweat out a confession" from him? But as we've seen this week, believers are urged to approach God's throne with boldness to confess their sins. Then, through Jesus' work on the cross, we receive forgiveness and purification, are freed from guilt and shame, and are called to hold fast to the hope that comes from knowing that God's promises are unshakable.

Confession lifts the weight of guilt and shame. When we acknowledge our need for forgiveness and receive God's mercy, we are freed to live in the confidence that we are loved, redeemed, and secure in Him. And when we confess, we are not just acknowledging our need for forgiveness—we are proclaiming that God's grace is greater than our sin and that His love is stronger than our guilt. As we bring our hearts before Him, we find not only forgiveness but also renewal and peace.

Confession is then followed by cleansing. The imagery in today's passage is rich and deeply tied to the Old Testament. The phrases "hearts sprinkled" and "bodies washed with pure water" evoke the ceremonial cleansing rituals of the Mosaic law. Under the old covenant, the high priest would sprinkle the blood of sacrifices to purify the people, while washing with water symbolized outward cleanliness. These rituals, however, were temporary and imperfect, pointing forward to a greater, eternal cleansing.

Jesus fulfilled what the old covenant could only foreshadow. Through His death, He offered Himself as the perfect sacrifice, cleansing not just our outer actions but our very consciences (Hebrews 9:13-14). No longer do we rely on the blood of animals; instead, we rest in the sufficiency of Jesus' blood, shed once for all (Hebrews 10:10).

Confession is the means by which we receive and experience this cleansing. As 1 John 1:9 assures us, "If we confess our sins, he is faithful and just to forgive us our sins and to purify us from all unrighteousness." When we come to God in confession, we are not met with condemnation but with mercy and grace. He doesn't just forgive; He restores and renews. I like Stormie Omartian's perspective on this: "It's not about finding ways to avoid God's judgment and feeling like a failure if you don't do everything perfectly. It's about fully experiencing God's love and letting it perfect you. It's not about being somebody you are not. It's about becoming who you really are."[20]

Confession not only cleanses us, it also leads us to hope. Hebrews 10:23 urges us to "hold unswervingly to the hope we profess, for he who promised is faithful." This type of hope is not just crossing your fingers, closing your eyes, and making a wish that things will go your way. Christian hope is rooted in the character of God and the certainty that because Jesus died for you and lives for you, you can depend on Him. Because He is faithful, we can trust that His promises will never fail.

This hope is not just for eternity; it is for today. We're not being defined by our failures but by God's grace, so we have the assurance that no matter how far we've strayed, His arms are always open, ready to welcome us back.

The goodness of God is evident in every aspect of confession and cleansing. It's His goodness that invites us to draw near, even when we feel unworthy. It's His goodness that assures us that His promises are trustworthy. And it's His goodness that fills us with hope, even in our darkest moments.

Reflect and Pray

1. Review Hebrews 10:21-23. How does being cleansed from a guilty/evil conscience encourage you to draw nearer to God?

2. How does God's faithfulness (Hebrews 10:23) give you hope in times of doubt or failure?

3. Review 1 John 1:9. Why is confession such an essential part of experiencing God's mercy and cleansing?

4. How would you describe your level of hope in the Lord? Is it much like making a birthday wish? A confident belief that God will act on your behalf? Or somewhere in between?

5. Reflect on the content of this week's devotionals. How are you seeing God's goodness and mercy in new (or stronger) ways? Thank Him for revealing himself to you.

God's Goodness as Our Refuge

Julie Clinton

I RECENTLY ATTENDED THE VIRGINIA CHRISTMAS SPECTACULAR at Thomas Road Baptist Church in Lynchburg. For more than fifty years now, this annual event has become a much-anticipated production in central Virginia. Each year brings a new creative presentation of the story of Jesus' birth that includes music, dance, and the legendary "Living Christmas Tree" that dates back to the earliest years of the program. Every year features a new theme, and I am struck by how, although past shows have featured various decades and locales from year to year, the program consistently gives the audience new insight into how to apply the meaning of Christmas to their daily lives.

For example, the 2023 theme, "Christmas on Route 66," transported audience members to Christmas Eve in 1956, when a group of strangers were stranded while traveling from Chicago to Los Angeles. They found themselves in Tannenbaum, a small New Mexico town where they shared meals, swapped stories, and found joy in the unlikeliest place. It was a poignant reminder that even when life doesn't go as planned, there is beauty to be found in the waiting.

Beyond the incredible vocals and powerful performances, there's something profoundly moving about the stories presented at the Virginia Christmas Spectacular each year. Each time I've attended, I've been reminded of my ultimate refuge in Jesus. So as we begin this week focusing on God's goodness as our refuge, I invite you to think about your own "Tannenbaum moments"—those times when life didn't go as you expected, but God showed up in surprising ways. Just as the travelers in the Christmas story found unexpected joy and connection, we can find hope, strength, and peace in the refuge of God's presence.

I hope you enjoyed Megan's insights on Hebrews last week. This week, I will discuss similar themes found in other portions of that challenging and meaningful book of Scripture. We will explore how God's mercy and goodness provide an anchor for our souls, a stronghold in trials, and a source of victory in life. We'll be challenged to fix our eyes on Jesus, our ultimate refuge. When we do, we will find rest in His unchanging goodness.

Finding Hope in God's Mercy

When God desired to show more convincingly to the heirs of the promise the unchangeable character of his purpose, he guaranteed it with an oath, so that . . . we who have fled for refuge might have strong encouragement to hold fast to the hope set before us. We have this as a sure and steadfast anchor of the soul.

HEBREWS 6:17-19

LIFE CAN OFTEN FEEL LIKE A STORMY SEA—unpredictable, overwhelming, and capable of terrifying even the strongest among us. But in today's passage we're reminded that God's mercy gives us hope that is unwavering and steadfast, like an anchor for the soul. This hope isn't just a fleeting wish on our part; it's a firm foundation rooted in God's promise and faithfulness.

Back in Week 1 (Day 3), I told you about a recent Alaskan cruise I took. But as much as I enjoyed the incredible beauty and diverse wildlife on that trip, there were other moments when I was almost as fascinated by the ship itself—particularly the anchor. Maybe, like me, you've been out on a boat with friends, and someone tosses the anchor overboard to prevent the boat from drifting around. But this was no little boat I was on; it was an enormous ship, and its anchor was massive! It had to be, of course, to grip the ocean floor and hold that large ship firmly, even if the waters began to rage (which I'm glad I didn't have to witness personally).

In the same way, our lives need an anchor capable of holding us steady when the waters are no longer serene and storms begin to brew. That anchor, as Hebrews tells us, is the hope we have in God's mercy and promises. Sometimes I wish God would be a little more specific about His plans for me, but I suspect that's how He is strengthening my hope in Him. I know He is still my refuge, even when I don't know exactly what's ahead for me. Anne Lamott reminds us that "Hope begins in the dark, the stubborn hope that if you just show up and try to do the right thing, the dawn will come. You wait and watch and work: You don't give up."[21] I also like what Joni Eareckson Tada says: "The best we can hope for in this life is a knothole peek at the shining realities ahead. Yet a glimpse is enough. It's enough to convince our hearts that whatever sufferings and sorrows currently assail us aren't worthy of comparison to that which waits over the horizon."[22]

Today's passage mentions those who have "fled for refuge . . . to hold fast to the hope set before us." This imagery refers to the cities of refuge established in the Old Testament (Numbers 35:6, 9-15). Those six cities (three on each side of the Jordan River) were places where someone accused of wrongdoing (particularly killing someone) could flee to receive a fair trial and justice. Anyone going to a city of refuge wasn't taking time to enjoy the scenery on the way—they were hastening to a place of safety as fast as they could go (before the victim's family members could exact their own revenge)! Similarly, we can urgently flee to God anytime we're overwhelmed, burdened, or broken.

God, in His mercy, welcomes us with open arms, providing a refuge that is unshaken by life's storms. He doesn't turn us away because of our failures or doubts; instead, He invites us to take hold of the hope He offers—a hope anchored in His unchanging character and promises. The author of Hebrews describes this hope as a "sure and stead-fast anchor for the soul." This metaphor paints a vivid picture of stability and peace, even in the midst of chaos. Just as an anchor holds a ship steady in turbulent waters, our hope in God keeps us grounded when life feels uncertain.

When was the last time you fled to God for refuge? Perhaps it's been a while. Maybe you're even carrying burdens that you haven't fully surrendered to Him. Let today be a reminder that His mercy is always available, always sufficient, and always ready to provide the safety and peace you need.

Reflect and Pray

1. What does it mean to you that God's promises are "guaranteed with [His] oath" (Hebrews 6:17)?

2. What are some promises of God that give you hope and encouragement during difficult times?

3. What burdens, if any, are you currently carrying that you haven't yet fully surrendered to God?

4. With no designated cities of refuge today, how do we "flee for refuge" to receive God's help?

5. Thank God for the way His promises act as an anchor to keep you grounded during challenging times.

Jesus, Our Refuge

**We have this as a sure and steadfast anchor of the soul,
a hope that enters into the inner place behind the curtain,
where Jesus has gone as a forerunner on our behalf.**

HEBREWS 6:19-20

IT'S A COMFORT TO KNOW YOU HAVE A REFUGE, a safe place to run to when life feels overwhelming.

Psalm 46:1 says, "God is our refuge and strength, an ever-present help in trouble." This verse perfectly captures what Hebrews has been affirming about Jesus. He is our refuge—not just in times of crisis, but in every moment of life. He invites us to bring our fears, doubts, and burdens to Him, knowing that He is more than capable of carrying them.

Yesterday we looked at hope as an anchor for the soul, a steadying force in the midst of life's storms. Today, Hebrews invites us to look even closer at this hope and the One who makes it possible—Jesus, our refuge and forerunner, who entered the inner sanctuary on our behalf.

When Hebrews speaks of the "inner sanctuary," it's referring to the Holy of Holies, the innermost part of the temple where God's presence dwelled. Under the old covenant, access to this sacred space was limited and conditional. Only the high priest could enter the Holy of Holies, and even then, only once a year on the Day of Atonement. But when Jesus died, the curtain of the temple was torn in two from top to bottom (Matthew 27:51). This occurred at a dramatic moment as the earth shook and rocks split. It was a declaration that the barrier between God and humanity had been removed by our perfect high priest. Through His sacrifice, Jesus made it possible for us to approach God directly, without fear or hesitation.

The word "forerunner" in Hebrews 6:20 (*prodromos* in Greek) is rich in meaning. A forerunner is someone who goes ahead to prepare the way for others. Interestingly, this is the only place in Scripture this Greek word is used! The imagery in this verse paints a beautiful picture of God's mercy and love. Jesus didn't just *create* a pathway to God—He *became* the pathway, ensuring that we can approach God confidently, knowing that He has gone before us.

Consider what this means for us today. Jesus isn't a distant Savior; He's intimately involved in our journey. He has already gone ahead, preparing the way for us to follow. He knows the path, the challenges, and the joys that lie ahead, and He walks with us every step of the way. Ladies, think about the comfort this brings. Whatever you face, you're not walking into the unknown alone. Jesus has already been there, and He promises to guide and sustain you. He is our refuge—our safe place and steady rock.

We don't have to strive or prove ourselves worthy to stand before God. Jesus has already done the work. His blood has cleansed us, His mercy has covered us, and His goodness invites us to draw near. Hebrews 10:19-22 (NIV) reminds us, "Therefore, brothers and sisters, since we have confidence to enter the Most Holy Place by the blood of Jesus . . . let us draw near to God with a sincere heart and with the full assurance that faith brings."

This confidence isn't about arrogance—it's about resting in the finished work of Christ. It's about trusting that Jesus, our forerunner, has made a way for us to experience the fullness of God's presence.

In a world where so many things feel uncertain, Jesus offers us a refuge that is unshakable. His promises are secure, His love is steadfast, and His presence is constant. Unlike earthly refuges that can fail or falter, Jesus is a stronghold that cannot be moved.

Jesus has already gone before us, preparing the way and making it possible for us to approach God with confidence. He is our refuge in every season of life, our steady anchor when the storms rage, and our greatest source of peace. As you reflect on today's passage, consider the ways Jesus has been your refuge and how you can rest more fully in His love.

Reflect and Pray

1. Reflect on Hebrews 6:19-20. How does the idea of Jesus as your forerunner encourage you in your faith journey?

2. What would the significance of the temple curtain being torn have meant to a first-century believer in God? What does it mean to you today?

3. What are some recent difficulties you've faced where you experienced Jesus as your refuge?

4. Do any barriers in your life prevent you from fully trusting Jesus as your refuge? How can you surrender them to Him?

5. Reflect in prayer on how the assurance of Jesus' finished work should increase your confidence to draw near to God.

Freedom through Mercy

If the blood of goats and bulls . . . sanctify for the purification of the flesh, how much more will the blood of Christ . . . purify our conscience from dead works to serve the living God.

HEBREWS 9:14

STUDIES SHOW THAT THE AVERAGE PERSON spends over two hours a day on social media, often comparing her life to highlight reels and curated posts. Research has linked excessive social media use to increased anxiety, depression, and feelings of inadequacy. We scroll endlessly, seeking connection, validation, or escape, only to find ourselves feeling more isolated and burdened than before. It's a perfect example of how we can chain ourselves to something that promises freedom but delivers the opposite.

Other than social media, what other invisible chains weigh you down and keep you from fully experiencing the life God intends for you? They may be emotional, mental, or spiritual burdens you've allowed to accumulate over time. Instead of embracing the freedom Christ offers, we often shackle ourselves to things that drain our joy and peace.

Hebrews 9:14 reminds us of the profound freedom available through Christ's mercy. His sacrifice cleanses our consciences, breaks the chains of sin and guilt, and liberates us to serve the living God. The first step to freedom is recognizing what's holding us back. Sometimes the chains are obvious—sins we struggle with, guilt from the past, or toxic relationships that weigh us down. Other times, the chains are subtle, such as the endless pursuit of perfection, the constant need for approval, striving for achievements that will never truly satisfy, or clinging to habits that leave us feeling empty.

Social media can be one of these subtle chains. While it can be a tool for connection and inspiration, it often becomes a source of distraction and discontentment. A study by the University of Pennsylvania found that reducing social media use to 30 minutes a day significantly decreased feelings of loneliness and depression. Yet, how often do we pick up our phones out of habit, tethering ourselves to a cycle of comparison and insecurity?

What are the chains in your life? The good news is that you don't have to live chained to those burdens. Hebrews 9:14 tells us that Christ's sacrifice cleanses our consciences from "dead works" so that we may serve the living God. His mercy doesn't just cover our sins; it frees us from the guilt, shame, and distractions that keep us from living fully for Him.

Think about how freeing that is. Jesus didn't just break the chains of sin—He shattered the barriers that keep us from experiencing His joy and peace. This is the kind of freedom the apostle Paul describes in Galatians 5:1: "For freedom Christ has set us free; stand firm therefore, and do not submit again to a yoke of slavery."

Are you living your life as if you are still chained? Are you clinging to old patterns, returning to the very things Christ died to free us from? The freedom Christ offers requires us to trust Him enough to let go—of sin, of guilt, and of anything that promises satisfaction but leaves us empty. Instead of turning to social media for validation, what if we turned to God's Word to remind us of our true identity? Instead of numbing our pain with distractions, what if we brought our struggles to Jesus, trusting Him to heal and restore us?

Freedom in Christ isn't just about letting go of chains; it's about stepping into the life He's called us to. Hebrews 9:14 tells us that this freedom enables us to "serve the living God." When we're no longer weighed down by guilt or striving, we're free to live with purpose, joy, and gratitude.

Imagine what it would look like to live fully in that freedom: to wake up each day unburdened by comparison, confident in who God created you to be . . . to use social media not as a source of validation but as a tool to encourage and uplift others . . . to spend your energy not on striving for perfection but on loving God and serving those around you.

Living in freedom doesn't mean life will be free of challenges, but it does mean we can face those challenges with confidence, knowing that we are deeply loved and fully equipped by God's grace. As Jesus said in John 8:36, "If the Son sets you free, you will be free indeed."

What chains are holding you back from fully experiencing the freedom Christ offers? Take some time today to identify those burdens and surrender them to God. Remember, His mercy has already secured your freedom. You don't have to live weighed down by guilt, shame, or distractions. Let go of the chains and step into the abundant life He has prepared for you.

Reflect and Pray

1. Review Hebrews 9:14. What does it mean that Christ's sacrifice cleanses your conscience?

2. What are some "chains" in your life that keep you from fully experiencing God's freedom?

3. How has social media or some other modern distraction impacted your spiritual life? How can you set healthier boundaries?

4. Reread Galatians 5:1. What does it look like to stand firm in the freedom Christ has given you?

5. Reflect today on how living in freedom can empower you to serve the living God more fully. Ask God to increase your faith and courage to live in that freedom.

Faith in Trials

Now faith is the assurance of things hoped for, the conviction of things not seen.

HEBREWS 11:1

SOME OF YOU HAVE HEARD my friend Margaret Feinberg speak at our EWomen conferences. Margaret is a gifted Bible teacher and writer who helps us see God's joy, goodness, and mercy, even in life's hardest moments. Recently, she spoke about practical ways to keep our minds focused on God rather than being overwhelmed by fear and anxiety. Margaret described how she determined what thoughts and phrases to focus on and repeat to stay centered on the truth. One of her reminders that really stuck with me was this: "I will serve the God who is above all else."

That simple practice has stayed with me, especially during times when life feels heavy. Inspired by Margaret, I've begun writing my own phrases to meditate on when I feel overwhelmed. They remind me to lift my eyes off my circumstances and focus instead on God's faithfulness. A few of them include:

> » "I will trust the God who keeps His promises."
> » "I will remember that God's mercies are new every morning."
> » "I will rest in the truth that God is working, even when I can't see it."

Faith is a not a passive feeling or blind optimism—it's an active confidence in God, even when we can't see the way ahead. Hebrews 11 reminds us that faith isn't about having all the answers; it's about trusting the One who holds them. It's about leaning into His goodness and promises, especially in the middle of trials. This was the experience described by Elisabeth Elliott in her personal spiritual development: "I realized that the deepest spiritual lessons are not learned by His letting us have our way in the end, but by His making us wait, bearing with us in love and patience until we are able to honestly pray what He taught His disciples to pray: Thy will be done."[23]

Hebrews 11 recounts a series of biblical characters whose lives were marked by trust in God. They weren't perfect people; they were ordinary men and women who chose to believe in an extraordinary God. (Just like our Extraordinary Women ministry, the "Extraordinary" comes from God.) Noah built an ark when there wasn't a cloud in the sky (Hebrews 11:7). Abraham left everything familiar to follow God's promise of a homeland he had never seen (Hebrews 11:8). You'll also find Sarah, Jacob, Joseph, Gideon, Samson, David, Samuel, and others. Their acts of faith remind us that trusting God requires stepping into the unknown with confidence that He will guide us. Their faith was never in their own strength—it was in God's ability to fulfill His promises.

Faith begins with trusting God at His word, even when circumstances seem impossible. It's the foundation that allows us to endure through life's storms. Hebrews 11:1 calls faith "the assurance of things hoped for, the conviction of things not seen." This confidence isn't rooted in our circumstances but in the unchanging character of God.

The faith of those in Hebrews 11 isn't about having an easier life. It's about trusting and holding on to God's goodness, even when the outcome is uncertain. Moses chose to identify with God's people rather than the fleeting treasures of Egypt because he realized a greater reward was ahead (Hebrews 11:24-26)—and when he made that choice, he didn't know what would come next.

I encourage you to read through Hebrews 11 and review the lives of all those imperfect people. Then consider how your life is similar to theirs. On one hand, you believe that God is good and you think you know what God wants you to do. On the other hand, you can't be sure what your future holds and you have no guarantees that everything will work out well. What will you do? It's your choice to make. And if you have faith, you'll make the right one.

Reflect and Pray

1. We sometimes tend to equate having faith in something with hoping it will happen. Why does the writer of Hebrews define faith as assurance and conviction of unseen things?

2. What do you know about God that the heroes of faith in the Old Testament had no way of knowing? (See Hebrews 11:13-16.) How does that additional information bolster your ability to put your faith in God?

3. Reflect on Margaret's phrase: "I will serve the God who is above all else." How can this perspective help you navigate your current challenges?

4. Take a moment to write a phrase or two that you can use to remind yourself of God's goodness and mercy.

5. Reflect today on how to have greater assurance of things hoped for and conviction of things not seen. Ask God to increase your confidence that He holds the future in His hands.

DAY 5

Looking to Jesus

**Let us also lay aside every weight,
and sin which clings so closely, and let us run with endurance
the race that is set before us, looking to Jesus,
the founder and perfecter of our faith.**

HEBREWS 12:1-2

WHEN I THINK ABOUT RUNNING A RACE, I picture the freedom of movement—light shoes, no heavy bag to carry, no unnecessary weight. A successful runner is one who has removed every hindrance that might slow her down or throw her off course. The writer of Hebrews uses this metaphor to remind us that, as Christians, we are running a spiritual race, and it's crucial to cast off anything that hinders our progress.

One of the most significant weights in today's world is distraction. We are never far from distractions. We carry portable ones with us in our pockets or purses—our phones. Social media, emails, endless notifications, and the 24/7 cycle of information can easily weigh us down, stealing time and attention from things that truly matter. A recent study found that the average person spends over three hours a day on their phone. If we're not careful, the constant scrolling can tether us to a cycle of comparison, anxiety, and dissatisfaction. Instead of fixing our eyes on Jesus, we find our gaze fixed on screens, consuming content that often leaves us feeling empty.

I'm not suggesting that technology is inherently bad. Social media can connect us with loved ones and spread messages of hope. But when it consumes more of our attention than God does, it becomes a weight, a problem, a distraction. We begin to measure our worth by likes and comments rather than by the love and grace of Christ. It's like trying to run a race with a heavy backpack strapped on—every step becomes harder, and the finish line seems farther away. That's why Jesus urges us to "seek first the kingdom of God and his righteousness" (Matthew 6:33), and then everything else we need will fall into its proper place.

To live victoriously, we must intentionally identify and remove our distractions. For some, this might mean setting boundaries—turning off notifications, limiting screen time, or carving out tech-free moments to focus on prayer and reflection. For others, it might mean reevaluating how social media aligns with our values. Are we using it to glorify God and build up others, or has it become a source of pride, envy, or escape?

I've found it helpful to ask myself: "Is this helping me run my race, or is it slowing me down?" It's a simple way to evaluate how I spend my time and energy. When I catch myself mindlessly scrolling, I try to redirect my focus to something more purposeful—reading Scripture, spending time with loved ones, or simply being still and present with God.

Remember, the race we're running isn't about perfection; it's about perseverance. Throwing off the weights of distraction doesn't happen overnight, but each step of faith brings us closer to the life of victory God has for us. With every choice to prioritize Him over the noise of the world, we experience more joy and freedom of running with endurance. Let's run this race together, free and focused, trusting in the One who has already won the victory for us.

Reflect and Pray

1. Currently, what "weights" or distractions in your life might be hindering your spiritual race? Why haven't you already done something about them?

2. Reflect on Matthew 6:33. Is "the kingdom of God and his righteousness" currently your top priority? If not, what priorities are ahead of them? How can you seek God's kingdom first, even amidst a busy or distracted world?

3. How has social media or technology affected your ability to focus on Jesus? What changes can you make?

4. How does knowing that Jesus is the "perfecter of faith" encourage you to keep running, even when it's hard?

5. Has the concept of God as your refuge made a difference (even today) in how you think about Him? In what way(s)? What practical steps can you take to create more space for Him in your daily routine? Ask God to change you from the inside out so that He is the most important priority in your life.

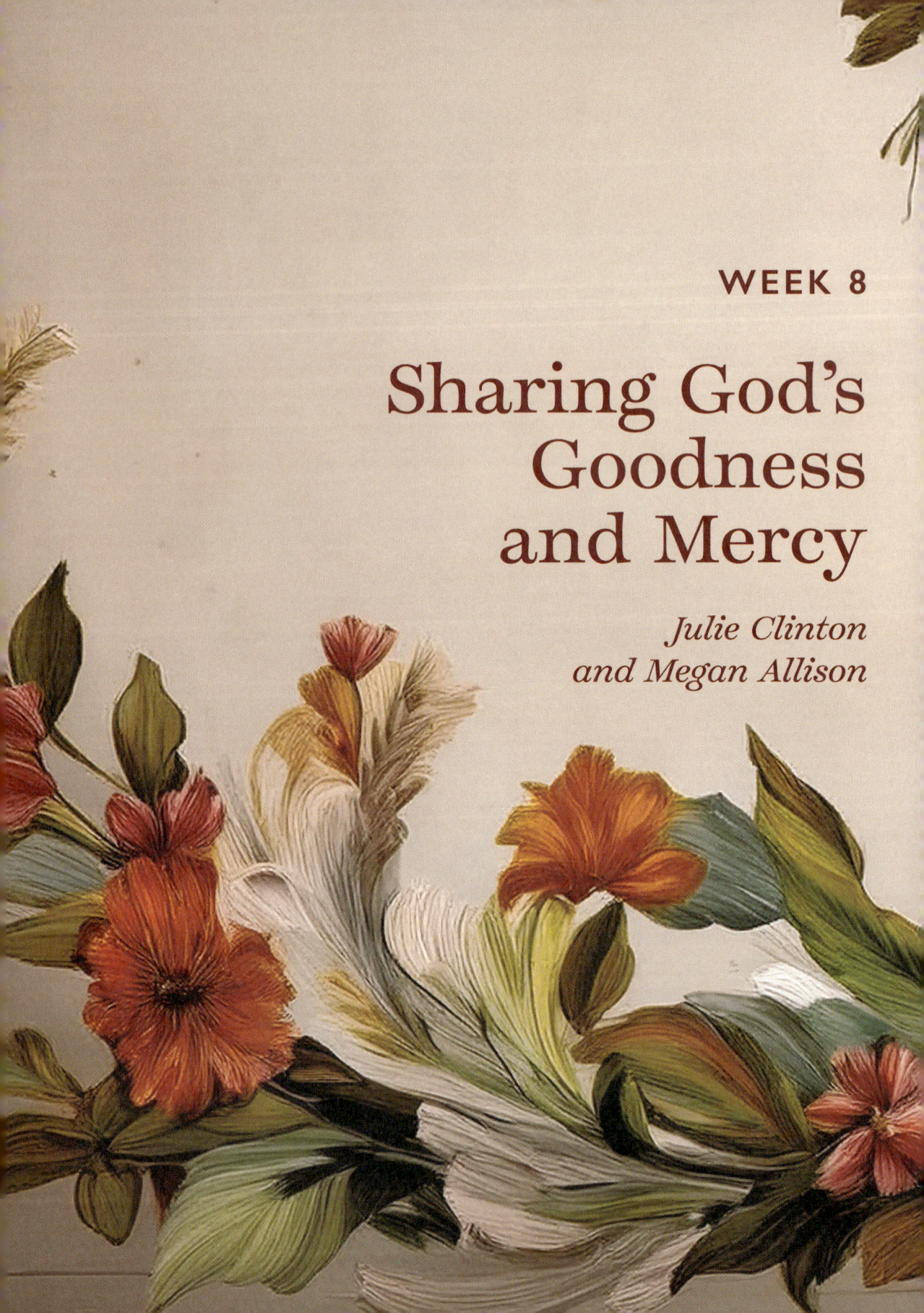

WEEK 8

Sharing God's Goodness and Mercy

Julie Clinton
and Megan Allison

From Megan:

We've covered a lot in the past seven weeks. From exploring God's mercy in our brokenness to understanding His goodness as our refuge, the journey has been filled with reminders of who God is and how deeply He cares for us. Each chapter has been an opportunity to pause, reflect, and draw closer to the One who meets us in every season of life.

For me, one of the most powerful truths has been that God's mercy isn't just a lifeline in hard times; it's the foundation of my daily walk with Him. You may have heard the expression often used to encourage moms of small children: "The days are long, but the years are short." The days can feel long because we're responsible for so many things, but we've seen how God's mercy sustains us, how His promises anchor us, and how His goodness empowers us to overcome challenges. The beauty of this journey doesn't end with our personal transformation. God's mercy and goodness are gifts meant to be shared.

As we enter the final week of our study, I'm struck by how God's mercy and goodness have been woven into every lesson we've shared. Reflecting on these truths has been a humbling and inspiring journey. This week takes us back to the book of Isaiah. We'll explore what it means to let what we've learned overflow into the lives of others. Isaiah's imagery of righteousness springing up like a garden reminds us that our faith was never meant to remain private—it's meant to impact our families, our communities, and even the world. Let's finish strong by focusing on how we can be vessels of His goodness and mercy, living lives that reflect His heart.

I'm sure you have had many people, tasks, and challenges call for your attention over the past seven weeks. I want to give you a big shout-out for sticking with this study and continuing to learn alongside us.

From Julie:

Looking back over all the Scripture we've studied, I've seen how each truth builds on the next, weaving a beautiful tapestry of God's love and faithfulness. We've seen that His mercy brings healing in brokenness, His goodness helps us overcome hardships, and His promises guide us through trials. I'm so glad we dug into the truths of

Hebrews together, reminding us of the great cloud of witnesses who lived by faith and pointed us to Jesus, the author and finisher of our faith.

In this final week, let's consider the significance of finishing well—not just this study but the race of faith we're all running. As we saw last week, Hebrews 12:1-2 reminds us to throw off everything that hinders us and fix our eyes on Jesus. That's the heart of this week: looking back on God's faithfulness with gratitude, looking around to encourage one another, and looking ahead to the joy set before us.

One of the most meaningful ways to finish well is by sharing what we've learned. Psalm 145:4 says, "One generation shall commend your works to another, and shall declare your mighty acts." Let's share God's goodness with others—not only the stories we've read in Scripture but also how we've experienced His mercy and love in our lives. Whether we share a testimony, lead a small group, or simply talk with a friend, those moments of reflection can have an eternal impact.

As we conclude this week, I want to thank you from the bottom of my heart for coming with us through this study. Megan and I are so grateful to have shared this journey with you, and we pray that this final chapter will inspire you to reflect on God's mercy and goodness with those around you. Let's finish strong, filled with gratitude for all He has done and hope for all that is yet to come.

Amazed at God's Sovereignty

"Remember the former things of old; for I am God,
and there is no other; I am God, and there is none like me,
declaring the end from the beginning and from ancient times
things not yet done, saying, 'My counsel shall stand,
and I will accomplish all my purpose.'"

ISAIAH 46:9-10

HAVE YOU EVER STOOD AT A CROSSROADS IN life and wished you could see what was ahead? Sometimes we assume it would be easier to trust God if we could get a glimpse of the twists and turns down the path, but through Isaiah, God reminds us that we don't need to see the future—we need to trust the One who already knows it and holds it in His hands. The book of Isaiah is often divided into two major sections: the first focusing on judgment (chapters 1-39) and the second on hope and redemption (chapters 40-66). In Isaiah 46, the prophet speaks to the exiled Israelites, reminding them of God's sovereignty over history and His power to fulfill His purposes, even in the face of overwhelming circumstances. He was asking them to trust Him even though their Temple had been destroyed, their homes burned and ransacked, thousands killed, and many more driven from their homes to a foreign land. It's easy to imagine they had trouble believing God was loving, wise, and kind! That's why God spoke these words of hope to them.

This passage in Isaiah reminds us of an essential truth we tend to forget when we feel overwhelmed by painful experiences: God sees the end from the beginning. He isn't bound by time or limited by circumstances. His purposes always prevail, even when the path forward seems unclear. Isaiah spoke during a time of political upheaval and spiritual decline, addressing the Assyrian threat and foretelling the Babylonian exile. Even in the middle of judgment, his message carried the promise of restoration, pointing to the ultimate hope in the coming Messiah. Isaiah's prophecies challenge us to trust

God's sovereignty and faithfulness because He alone can fulfill His purposes, no matter the obstacles.

Let's fast-forward and peek into the future that Isaiah didn't know was coming. The chapters of Esther span approximately ten years, beginning in 483 b.c. during the reign of King Xerxes (Ahasuerus) and concluding around 473 b.c. Esther lived during the Persian Empire's rule after the Jewish exile to Babylon and the return of the exiles under leaders like Zerubbabel and Ezra, though not all Jews returned to Jerusalem. Some, as we see in this account, were still living in Persia. Esther's testimony represents a moment when God preserved His people in exile, ensuring the survival of the Jewish lineage that would ultimately bring forth Jesus, the Messiah.

Isaiah, writing centuries earlier (circa 740–681 b.c.), prophesied to the people of Judah during the reigns of kings Hezekiah and Uzziah. Isaiah's message included warnings of exile as well as promises of restoration and hope through a coming Savior. When Esther became queen, the Jewish people were scattered, but they were still under God's covenant care. Together, Isaiah and Esther remind us of God's sovereignty in preserving His people. Esther's courage helped secure the continuation of the Jewish people, while Isaiah's prophetic vision pointed forward to their ultimate Redeemer, Jesus Christ, fulfilling God's promise to Abraham that through his seed, all nations would be blessed.

Esther, a beautiful young Jewish woman living in exile, was elevated to the position of queen in a pagan empire—not by chance, but by divine design. She had no idea she would play a crucial role in rescuing God's people from evil and destruction. In Esther 4:14, Mordecai challenges her with these profound words: "And who knows but that you have come to your royal position for such a time as this?" This pivotal moment reveals that Esther's position was part of God's plan to save His people from annihilation.

As we study Esther's story, we see God's hand at work, even in situations that seem beyond control. The king's sleepless night (Esther 6:1), Haman's downfall (Esther 7:10), and the bold courage Esther displayed in approaching the king (Esther 5:1-3) weren't mere coincidences. Though God's name is never mentioned in the book of Esther, His presence is unmistakable, reminding us that He is always working behind the scenes, even when He seems silent.

This story teaches us that trusting in God's sovereignty doesn't mean understanding every detail; it means believing that He is faithful to His promises. Esther's courage wasn't rooted in knowing how everything would unfold—it was grounded in her trust that God had placed her in her position for a purpose. Her obedience and faith became the conduit for God to rescue the Jewish people from Haman's plot to murder all of them.

At the end of Esther, God's people have a feast of celebration called Purim. The annual feast is still held today to remind generations far removed from the historic events that God worked intricately and powerfully to save His people. Each generation shares the story with the next one, reinforcing memory and faith. In the same way, God wants us to rehearse the wonders of His goodness and mercy to the next generation and to everyone we know. Don't forget the impact of God's presence and power in the past. Remember it and share it with others. When we focus on God's sovereignty and remember that He knows every twist and turn of our journey, it is easier to take our focus off of our own circumstances and remember to be a light to others, wherever we are.

Reflect and Pray

1. Read Isaiah 46:9-10. How does reflecting on God's sovereignty and His ability to "declare the end from the beginning" bring you peace in your current challenges?

2. Read Esther 4:14. How does Mordecai's encouragement to Esther challenge you to trust that God has a purpose for your season of life?

3. How does the connection between Isaiah's prophecy of restoration and Esther's role in preserving God's people inspire you to believe God has a plan even if you don't see it?

4. Consider a time when you couldn't see the outcome of a situation but later saw God's hand at work. How does this memory encourage you to trust Him now?

5. Ask God for an opportunity to share memories of God's sovereignty with someone near you.

DAY 2

Fruitful in God's Goodness and Mercy

For as the soil makes the sprout come up and a garden causes seeds to grow, so the Sovereign Lord will make righteousness and praise spring up before all nations.

ISAIAH 61:11

I (JULIE) LOVE TO SEE A FLOURISHING GARDEN. It begins with just a handful of seeds, buried and unseen, but over time—with the proper care and conditions—they transform into something vibrant and life-giving. If you are a mom, you might remember your child bringing home a seed planted in some dirt in a Styrofoam cup and then watching their utter delight when a little sprout broke through the surface! Isaiah uses the image of a garden to describe how God works in our lives, cultivating righteousness and praise that will ultimately glorify Him. Like a master gardener, God intentionally nurtures us, providing everything we need to grow and thrive in His goodness.

Jesus adds another layer of understanding to this imagery in John 15:1-5. He describes himself as the vine, we are branches connected to the vine, and God is the gardener. Our role is to remain connected to Him, allowing His life to flow through us and produce good fruit. But this growth doesn't happen overnight. It requires surrender, trust, patience, and a willingness to let God shape us. Like branches in a vineyard that must be pruned and watered, our hearts must remain open to His guidance and care.

We want to see growth, and we're often impatient with the Gardener! In *The Practice of Godliness*, Jerry Bridges encourages us to see delays as God's way of drawing us close: "The fruit of patience in all its aspects—long-suffering, forbearance, endurance, and perseverance—is a fruit that is most intimately associated with our devotion to God.

All character traits of godliness grow out of and have their foundation in our devotion to God, but the fruit of patience must grow out of that relationship in a particular way."[24]

God's mercy is like the life-giving water that sustains a garden through droughts. Without it, we would wither, and we would remain barren and fruitless. But His mercy transforms us, nourishing us in ways we don't always see or understand. Ephesians 2:4-5 reminds us of this truth: "But God, being rich in mercy, because of the great love with which he loved us, even when we were dead in our trespasses, made us alive together with Christ—by grace you have been saved."

Mercy enables us to grow in God's goodness, not because we deserve it but because He delights in making us flourish. Even when we feel unworthy or broken, His mercy meets us where we are, renewing and strengthening us for the journey. Think about the moments when God's mercy carried you through difficult seasons. Those are the times when He worked beneath the surface, preparing you for greater growth and fruitfulness.

The difficulties we face are times of pruning. Gardeners don't prune productive vines because they're upset with them and want to hurt them; the pruning is to maximize their potential for fruitfulness. Pruning isn't pleasant, but it's essential.

The ultimate purpose of our growth is to glorify God. Just as a beautiful garden draws admiration and points to the gardener's skill, our lives should reflect God's goodness and mercy to those around us. Isaiah 61:11 reminds us that the righteousness and praise God cultivates in us aren't just for our benefit—they are meant to spring up to nourish neighbors and nations, drawing others into His grace.

Jesus highlights this in Matthew 5:16, saying, "Let your light shine before others, that they may see your good deeds and glorify your Father in heaven." When we live in a way that reflects God's love and mercy, we become a testimony of His transformative power. This doesn't mean we have to be perfect—it means allowing His goodness to shine through our actions, words, and struggles.

As we said at the end of last week, distraction is one of the biggest obstacles to reflecting God's glory. Any number of things can capture our attention and turn our thoughts away from how good and merciful the Lord has been to us. Overcoming distractions takes intention and practice. We must be intentional about how we spend our time and what we focus on. Perhaps this means setting aside time each day to be still before God, or finding ways to serve others, letting His love flow through us in tangible acts of kindness and generosity.

Reflecting God's glory isn't about striving or performing—it's about staying connected to the vine and allowing His Spirit to work through us. Second Corinthians 5:20 reminds us, "We are ambassadors for Christ, God making his appeal through us." When we walk in His goodness and mercy, our lives become a living testimony of His love, pointing others to the hope and restoration found in Him.

Take a moment today to consider how you can experience and reflect God's goodness and mercy more fully. What distractions might you need to let go of? How can you align your actions, words, and thoughts with His purposes? Remember, God is the gardener, and He is faithful to bring growth and fruitfulness in His time. Trust Him to make righteousness and praise spring up in your life, drawing others to His glory.

Reflect and Pray

1. Read Isaiah 61:11. What does the imagery of a garden teach you about God's role in your spiritual growth?

2. Read John 15:1-5. What specific ways can you stay connected to Jesus, the true vine, in your daily life?

3. As you look back on your life, how has God pruned you? How did you interpret the pain at the time? How do you see it now?

4. What distractions keep you from fully experiencing God's goodness and mercy? What's the impact on you and your connection with Jesus, and with other people.

5. Invite God to prune you so you'll be more fruitful.

Sharing Shelter and Strength

You have been a refuge for the poor, a refuge for the needy in their distress, a shelter from the storm and a shade from the heat. For the breath of the ruthless is like a storm driving against a wall.

ISAIAH 25:4, NIV

LIFE HAS A WAY OF THROWING STORMS at us when we least expect them. These storms may come in the form of financial struggles, health challenges, family tension, or the weight of emotional burdens. During these times, we often feel exposed, vulnerable, and alone. Isaiah reminds us of a comforting truth: God is our refuge. He is the One who stands as a steadfast shelter, providing strength and safety in the midst of life's fiercest trials.

The concept of refuge is a beautiful thread throughout Scripture, and that image has come up in this book a few times already. In today's passage, the prophet reminds us that God has been a refuge for the poor and the needy—not just in one moment, but over and over again. In the Beatitudes, Jesus said, "Blessed are the poor in spirit." This means those humble enough realize they need to depend on God instead of themselves. What an incredible picture of God's faithfulness! His shelter isn't temporary or conditional; it's constant, steady, and unchanging. Whatever you're facing today, draw strength from this: God is a refuge for you. You can run to Him, knowing He will never turn you away.

People are fickle, and loyalties change, but "Jesus Christ is the same yesterday and today and forever" (Hebrews 13:8). Through the storms, God's character remains strong, faithful, and unwavering.

I think about the times I've seen God's consistency in my own life. No matter how often I've come to Him, He has never failed to provide the shelter I needed. This is a truth worth remembering, especially when life feels unsteady.

Isaiah doesn't promise that we'll never face storms. Instead, they point to God's presence as our shelter while we endure them. Trials are inevitable, but so is God's protection. Just as shade offers relief from the heat, God's presence gives us rest when life feels overwhelming.

One of my favorite passages of Scripture beautifully echoes this promise: "The Lord will keep you from all harm. He will watch over your life; the Lord will watch over your coming and going both now and forevermore" (Psalm 121:7-8). The "harm" in this passage doesn't refer to every setback and heartache; instead, it means God will protect us from being overwhelmed by difficulties. God's watchful care will sustain us through whatever we face.

Think about the storms you've faced, those moments when you felt certain you wouldn't make it through. Now, consider how God was a shelter for you. His shelter doesn't promise ease, but it guarantees His faithful presence, steady and unchanging, through it all.

When we experience God as our refuge, we gain the wisdom and sensitivity to explain how He is a refuge for others who are under stress. Just as God comforts us in our need, He calls us to extend that comfort to those around us.

In the opening verses in his second letter to the Corinthian Christians, Paul intimates that he had been under so much strain that he thought he was going to die. But even then, God was his refuge. He explained, "[God] comforts us in all our troubles, so that we can comfort those in any trouble with the comfort we ourselves receive from God" (2 Corinthians 1:4, NIV). God doesn't just meet us in our struggles for our sake; He equips us to bring hope and encouragement to others.

I recently met with a family friend who had been through a particularly challenging season of grief. As we talked, she shared how meaningful it had been to receive small gestures of kindness during her storm: a thoughtful note, a meal delivered, or a listening ear. These acts of love, she said, felt like glimpses of God's shelter during a time when she felt exposed to life's harsh elements.

You and I have the opportunity to be that glimpse of God's refuge for others. Perhaps it's a coworker who's struggling with burnout or a friend walking through a difficult diagnosis. Maybe it's as simple as offering a word of encouragement to someone who feels unseen. By sharing God's love and comfort, we "pay forward" the shelter we've received from Him.

What is our hope? Is it temporary relief or something more? In *Walking with God through Pain and Suffering*, author and pastor Tim Keller gives us a much bigger picture: "Christianity offers not merely a consolation but a restoration—not just of the life we had but of the life we always wanted but never achieved. And because the joy will be even greater for all that evil, this means the final defeat of all those forces that would have destroyed the purpose of God in creation, namely, to live with his people in glory and delight forever."[25]

Today's passage in Isaiah invites us to rest in the unchanging refuge of God. He is our shelter in the storm, our shade in the heat, and our strength in weakness—and someday, every wrong will be made right. But this truth isn't just for us. Who in your life needs to know about God's faithful presence? It's not about having a big budget to spend or making grand gestures; it's about the simple kindness of being a channel of God's love. Even the smallest act of care can make a lasting impact when it reflects His goodness.

Reflect and Pray

1. Read Isaiah 25:4. How has God been a shelter for you in one or more of your life's storms?

2. Reflect on Hebrews 13:8. How does God's unchanging nature comfort you during uncertain times?

3. What does finding "shade" in God's presence mean when life feels overwhelming?

4. Read 2 Corinthians 1:4. Who in your life might need to experience God's comfort and love?

5. Ask God to show you one person who needs to experience the comfort you've received from God.

Christmas Every Day?

**The people who walked in darkness have seen a great light . . .
For to us a child is born, to us a son is given; and the
government shall be upon his shoulder, and his name shall
be called Wonderful Counselor, Mighty God,
Everlasting Father, Prince of Peace.**

ISAIAH 9:1, 6

WHEN MEGAN AND ZACH WERE IN MIDDLE AND HIGH SCHOOL, one of our family's favorite holiday traditions was filling shoeboxes for Operation Christmas Child. Every year, our church joined churches around the nation assembling shoeboxes packed with toys, hygiene items, and school supplies to send to children in need around the world.

I (Julie) remember watching Megan and Zach carefully shop for the items for their boxes, deliberating over whether a soccer ball or a doll would bring more joy, or how many crayons could fit in the box next to a coloring book. They'd write notes to the kids who would receive their gifts. Their sheer excitement in envisioning the joy their small efforts would bring someone else was a beautiful reminder that even from a young age, we can sense the connection to God that comes when we bless others. In those moments, they were participating in the kind of worship God desires: an outpouring of His love through tangible acts of service.

I think I had this family flashback for a couple of reasons: primarily because today's Scripture from Isaiah 9 is read so often at Christmas, but also because Megan and I were coming to the end of this study of God's goodness and mercy. We've both noted several times during these past weeks that God sometimes seems to keep us in the dark about what's ahead in our lives, expecting us to trust Him to see us through as He walks beside us day by day. We said that it can be more than a little frustrating for us at times, but it's how we build our faith because we can put great confidence in Him. Yet it makes me wonder how much more challenging it must have been for those who lived *before* the incarnation of Jesus and the coming of the Holy Spirit—those who could only watch and wait for a more personal God, for the privilege of coming before Him boldly to ask for His mercy, and who must have questioned His goodness as they faced war, defeat, despair, exile, and other physical and emotional crises.

Yes, we've seen flashes of light and hope amid their struggles. We saw the list of heroes of faith recorded in Hebrews 11. We saw Esther's rise to become Queen of Persia at just the right time to save her people from extinction. And we've seen other glimpses of exceptional faith and hope—all before the arrival of Jesus.

However, today's Scripture was only a prophecy for the first people who heard it—a promise that wouldn't be fulfilled for centuries. But after it *was* fulfilled, oh, just think what a difference Jesus' incarnation has made for us. Each of His titles is a promise in itself. When we're stuck or confused, our Wonderful Counselor is on call to advise us about what's best in our lives. When we feel like we just can't go on any longer, our always-accessible Mighty God empowers us. If we're feeling unloved or outcast, we'll find our Everlasting Father running to meet and embrace us, as the Prodigal Son's father did for him. And whenever we're hassled, conflicted, nervous, or otherwise unsettled, the Prince of Peace can provide a sense of contentment beyond human understanding.

God's wisdom, might, counsel, and peace are all part of His goodness and mercy. And His goodness and mercy both derive from His love. Now that Jesus has come, all those benefits are here to stay. The verse that follows today's Scripture promises: "Of the increase of his government and of peace there will be no end, on the throne of David and over his kingdom, to establish it and to uphold it with justice and with righteousness from this time forth and forevermore. The zeal of the Lord of hosts will do this" (Isaiah 9:7).

That means there's no expiration date on God's promises. We've seen that "his mercies never come to an end; they are new every morning" (Lamentations 3:22-23). So why do so many of us wait until Christmas to center our thoughts on godly priorities: peace on earth . . . showing goodwill to one another . . . being nice instead of naughty? What if more of us acknowledged every day that the Jesus we serve was/is the embodiment of God's unfathomable goodness and mercy, and then treated other people better in response? That's what He taught us. That's what He modeled for us. And that's what He died to prove to us. If more of us would take that truth to heart in our thoughts, words, and actions, and then treat one another with that awareness, don't you think every day would feel more like Christmas?

Jesus was a great light sent to people living in darkness. That light still shines. Let it ignite in your own heart until others see it and are drawn to it.

Reflect and Pray

1. Envision yourself as an Old Testament believer in God under the law of Moses. How would you try to ensure that He was pleased with you? How could you be sure? What do you think would be your greatest concerns and challenges?

2. Why do you think so many people today tend to be drawn to church or religious services only rarely, but especially at Christmas and Easter? What keeps them from attending more frequently?

3. What are some ways that even committed believers can sometimes just "go through the motions" of service to others without engaging our hearts?

4. How do you most typically relate to Jesus: as a Wonderful Counselor? A Mighty God? An Everlasting Father? Or a Prince of Peace? How can you more fully experience all four aspects?

5. List all of the benefits/freedoms you have in your relationship with God because of Jesus' birth, life, death, and resurrection. Ask God to make you more aware and appreciative of these blessings on a daily basis.

An Open Invitation

Seek the Lord while he may be found; call upon him while
he is near. Let the wicked forsake their ways and the
unrighteous their thoughts. Let them turn to the Lord, and
he will have mercy on them, and to our God,
for he will freely pardon.

ISAIAH 55:6-7, NIV

You may have noticed that as we've gotten closer to the end of this study, your two authors have devoted a lot of attention to the insights found in the book of Isaiah. And we've tried to save the best for last. Yesterday we considered what a difference the incarnation of Jesus should make both in our personal lives and in our relationships—blessings that we can experience that were still unavailable to Old Testament believers.

Today, however, we're looking at an invitation that is timeless. It was first made to those Old Testament Israelites, but it's just as valid for us today. In addition to today's verse, Isaiah 55 is packed with other powerful insights and promises. Here are a few:

> » "Come, everyone who thirsts, come to the waters; and he who has no money, come, buy and eat! Come, buy wine and milk without money and without price" (v. 1).

> » "For my thoughts are not your thoughts, neither are your ways my ways, declares the Lord. For as the heavens are higher than the earth, so are my ways higher than your ways and my thoughts than your thoughts" (vv. 8-9).

> » "You shall go out in joy and be led forth in peace; the mountains and the hills before you shall break forth into singing and all the trees of the field shall clap their hands" (v. 12).

God appears to be doing everything possible to eliminate all our excuses. It's like He's saying, "In My goodness, I'm offering you everything you could possibly need . . . at no charge. You may wonder how or why I would do such a thing, but don't worry about it because My ways are so different from your ways that you can't fully understand. I know some of you feel guilty for things you've done, and you may even be afraid of Me. Don't worry about that either, because I am merciful and will freely forgive you. All I ask is that you forsake your unrighteous ways and turn to Me. If you do, you will experience real peace and joy in your life."

It sounds too easy, doesn't it? But honestly, it can indeed feel intimidating when you realize you're standing in the presence of God. You might remember that Moses at the burning bush was a hard sell on responding to God's call, quickly citing five different excuses why God should look elsewhere for a different volunteer (Exodus 3:1-4:17). But when he finally yielded to God's call, things worked out quite well (though not necessarily easily) for Moses and his people.

We also need to note that after the opening invitation for people to come to Him and receive everything they need at no charge, God asks a poignant question in Isaiah 55: "Why do you spend your money for that which is not bread, and your labor for that which does not satisfy?" (v. 2). Centuries later, Jesus would ask the same question of those listening to (and later reading) His Sermon on the Mount. He asks us all:

> "Is not life more than food, and the body more than clothes? Look at the birds of the air; they do not sow or reap or store away in barns, and yet your heavenly Father feeds them . . . And why do you worry about clothes? See how the flowers of the field grow. They do not labor or spin. Yet I tell you that not even Solomon in all his splendor was dressed like one of these . . . So do not worry, saying, 'What shall we eat?' or 'What shall we drink?' or 'What shall we wear?' For the pagans run after all these things, and your heavenly Father knows that you need them. But seek first his kingdom and his righteousness, and all these things will be given to you as well." (Matthew 6:25-26, 28-29, 31-33)

As we close this eight-week look at God's goodness and mercy, we'll leave you with God's promise and His question. Isaiah 55 is essentially the Old Testament version of Philippians 4:19: "My God will meet all your needs according to the riches of his glory in Christ Jesus." First, let that truth sink in. If you have doubts or excuses that keep you from "coming to the waters," express them to God honestly and listen patiently for His response. Talk to a trusted counselor if you'd like. And then, when you're ready, consider the question: "Why do you spend your money for that which is not bread, and your labor for that which does not satisfy?"

If you remember nothing else from this study, we hope you never forget that God's goodness is the source of everything good in your life and that you can strengthen your relationship with Him as you better comprehend that truth. Likewise, know that you can never do anything so terrible that it can't be forgiven in His great mercy. He is eager to restore every broken relationship. And as your own life is increasingly bolstered by the goodness and mercy of God, you'll be much better equipped to help others—especially those you love.

You're not on your own, you know. God will equip you with His Spirit and surround you with a community of believers to encourage, pray for, and walk alongside you. If you don't have a community of believers like that, reach out to find one—or cultivate one.

Also know that we are praying for you to keep loving others, keep showing up, and keep trusting that God will use your faithfulness to make an impact far beyond what you can see. Whether it's a small gesture like sharing a smile or a larger act of service, your compassion makes a difference. Take heart, friend, and press on, knowing that God is working through you to bring His love into a world that desperately needs it.

We will conclude this study much as we began it, with one more reminder for you: "Surely [God's] goodness and mercy shall follow you all the days of your life."

Reflect and Pray

1. Read Isaiah 55 straight through. (It's not long.) What statements stand out most for you?

2. What excuses have you used in the past to avoid a more committed relationship with God? Are you currently making excuses?

3. We've previously considered distractions that sometimes take priority over our relationships with God and others, but Jesus suggests that even our food and clothing can become distractions. How have you seen that to be true?

4. How is today's invitation to get your own life in order the first step in this week's theme of "Sharing God's Goodness and Mercy"?

5. Reflect on the content of the previous eight weeks. What truths stand out most in your mind? What will you do to apply them in the weeks to come? Who do you know who desperately needs to experience more of God's goodness and mercy? Ask God to give you the right time, the right place, and the right words to share with your friend.

Endnotes

1. Brennan Manning, *The Ragamuffin Gospel: Good News for the Bedraggled, Beat-Up, and Burnt Out* (Colorado Springs: Multnomah, 2008), p. 68.

2. John Bowlby, *Attachment* (New York: Basic Books, 1969).

3. Tim Keller, *Every Good Endeavor* (New York: Penguin Books, 2012), p. 23.

4. Charles C. Ryrie, *Basic Theology: A Popular Systematic Guide to Understanding Biblical Truth* (Chicago: Moody Publishers, 1999), Chapter 6.

5. Charles Haddon Spurgeon, *"Spurgeon at His Best: Over 2200 Striking Quotations from the World's Most Exhaustive and Widely-Read Sermon Series"* (Ada, MI: Baker Publishing Group, 1988).

6. Anne Lamott, *Hallelujah Anyway: Rediscovering Mercy*, cited at https://theinwardturn.com/hallelujah-anyway-anne-lamott-on-extending-and-receiving-mercy-in-a-broken-world/

7. Henri Nouwen, *On Solitude* (Notre Dame, IN: Ave Maria Press, 2004), p. 38.

8. C. S. Lewis, "The Weight of Glory," a sermon delivered in Church of St. Mary the Virgin, Oxford, June 8, 1942, https://www.doxaweb.com/assets/weight_of_glory.pdf

9. Gerald May, *The Awakened Heart* (New York: HarperCollins, 1993).

10. Richard Abanes, *Rick Warren and the Purpose that Drives Him* (Eugene, OR: Harvest House, 2005), p. 65.

11. Augustine, *Sermons* 191.1

12. Thomas Manton, *The Complete Works of Thomas Manton*, 2:340-341.

13. Miroslav Volf, *Exclusion and Embrace* (Nashville: Abingdon Press, 1996), p. 124.

14. Lewis Smedes, *Forgive and Forget*, (New York: Harper & Row, 1984), pp. 79-80.

15. Tim Keller, *The Reason for God* (New York: Penguin, 2009), p. 196.

16. Jack Frost, *Experiencing the Father's Embrace* (Destiny Publishers, 2006), p. 191.

17. Lewis Smedes, *The Art of Forgiving: When You Need To Forgive And Don't Know How* (New York: Ballantine Books, 1996), p. 171.

18. Max Lucado, "Trusting More, Worrying Less," https://maxlucado.com/trusting-more-worrying-less/

19. Paul David Tripp, *New Morning Mercies: A Daily Gospel Devotional* (Wheaton: Crossway, 2014), p. 21.

20. Stormie Omartian, *The Power of a Praying Woman* (Nashville: Thomas Nelson, 1982), p. 33.

21. Anne Lamott, *Bird by Bird* (New York: Random House, 1994), p. xxiii.

22. Joni Eareckson Tada, cited in *Inspired Faith* (Nashville: Thomas Nelson, 2012), p. 93.

23. Elisabeth Elliott, *Passion and Purity: Learning to Bring Your Love Life Under Christ's Control* (New York: Revell, 1984).

24. Jerry Bridges, *The Practice of Godliness* (Colorado Springs:NavPress, 1996), p. 179.

25. Tim Keller, *Walking with God through Pain and Suffering* (New York: Penguin Group: 2013), p. 159.

Acknowledgments

We are deeply grateful to the individuals who helped bring this Bible Study to life.

A heartfelt thank you to Dina Jones for joining with us to craft this work. You are a treasure.

To Pat Springle, Stan Campbell, Anne McLaughlin, and Kimberly Bailey, for your thoughtful editing, wise counsel, and beautiful design.

To Jennifer Ellers, your expertise and encouragement have been a gift. We're so thankful for the care and creativity you have poured into this project and everything you do.

Garrett Hedrick, your dedication and passion for every event and endeavor continue to inspire us. Thank you for your unwavering support and kindness. Thank you to Kim and the whole team for your creativity and spirit of excellence.

To Beth Peterson and the EWomen Team, thank you for choosing to join us in ministry. You bless so many lives with your hard work and obedience to your calling.

Thank you to our Pastor, Jonathan Falwell, the pastoral team, and church community at Thomas Road Baptist Church. We are so thankful to have a church so deeply rooted in the Word.

From Julie: Megan, sharing the Extraordinary Women ministry with you is one of my life's greatest blessings. My heart overflows with gratitude for our special bond and the opportunity to work together.

Tim, your love and friendship mean everything to me. I thank God every day for the life we share and for the privilege of raising Megan and Zach with you.

From Megan: Mom, your daily walk with Jesus has been a constant example and encouragement to me. Watching my daughters Olivia and Sophia be shaped by your love and wisdom is one of the greatest joys of my life.

Ben, you bring so much laughter and light into our days. Sharing this life and parenting journey with you is a gift beyond measure. I love you with all my heart.

About the Authors

Julie Clinton, M.Ad, MBA, is President of Extraordinary Women Ministries. She has spoken to hundreds of thousands of women as host of Extraordinary Women conferences all across America and has authored five books. A woman of deep faith, she cares passionately about seeing women live out their dreams by finding their freedom in Christ. Julie and her husband, Tim, live in Virginia and have two adult children, Megan (married to Ben) and Zach (married to Evelyn). Julie is "GiGi" to Megan's daughters, Olivia and Sophia.

Megan Allison, PA-C, D.MSc., is a seasoned dermatology practitioner. She enjoys public speaking and education, and she is a published author of four books. She is a member of the American Academy of Physician Assistants (AAPA) and the Society of Dermatology Physician Assistants (SDPA). Megan received her Master's Degree in Physician Assistant Studies from Jefferson College of Health Sciences in Roanoke, Virginia. She received her Doctor of Medical Science Degree from the University of Lynchburg where she completed additional training in general and pediatric dermatology. Megan is married to her high school sweetheart, Ben, and together they have fun raising their daughters Olivia and Sophia.

Dina Jones, M.A. is the Director of Publications for the International Christian Coaching Association (ICCA) and a Board-Certified Professional Christian Life Coach. She is also in her tenth year of teaching as an adjunct instructor for Liberty University's College of Arts and Sciences. She is married to Jesse and has three children: Mackenzie, Madison, and Alexander.

Resources

To order these books,
go to Amazon.com or www.aacc.net

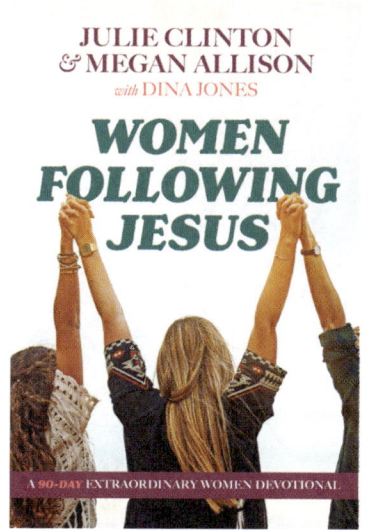

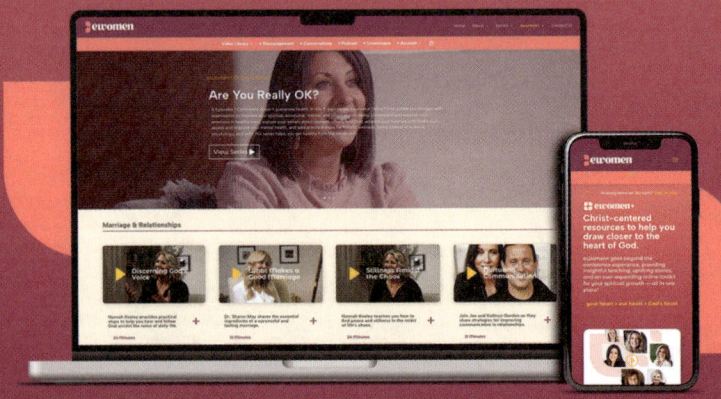